'Dr. Yeonkwon Jung's book, *Korean Business Communication*, is a must-read for educators, researchers, and practitioners interested in Korean business communication with its unique insights drawn from both theory and practice. Theoretically, it goes beyond the sophisticated stereotypes of culture to revisit and define Korean business communication from an in-depth local cultural perspective. Practically, Korean business communication genres are explored to reflect not only discourse competence but also, more importantly, the sociolinguistic and strategic competence most essential for local and global business success.'

Yunxia Zhu, the University of Queensland

'Dr. Jung's seminal work on Korean business communication is a balanced overview of theories and practices of Korean business communication with well-selected relevant studies. This is well researched and will be very useful to those working in business discourse, pragmatic studies, and communication studies. Readers will gain insights not only on Korean business communication but also on cross-cultural business communication.'

Jihyeon Jeon, Ewha Womans University,
Immediate Past President of Asia TEFL

Korean Business Communication

Korean Business Communication demonstrates the heuristic value of the research on Korean business communication.

It is composed of two parts: theory and practice. First, alongside the review of the major research trend of Asian business communication, it explores the contemporary teaching trend of business communication in Korean higher education to define business communication from the local perspective. It also shows how Korean business professionals manage facework within the communication rules or cultural values. Second, Korean business communication data are analyzed with the main sources of three types of competence: discourse competence, sociolinguistic competence, and strategic competence. Emphasis is on stakeholder communication genres, Korean service encounters, Korean business apology, and Korean CEO's online greetings.

By examining how business communication and Korean communication are projected to Korean business, *Korean Business Communication* provides the audience with knowledge far beyond cultural stereotypes in Korean business communication illustrated in classical textbooks on Korean business communication. It is a useful textbook for students in courses on Asian business communication, intercultural communication, and global communication.

Yeonkwon Jung is Professor of Business Communication at Kansai Gaidai University (KGU). Prior to joining KGU, he held numerous teaching and research appointments, including positions in the Helsinki School of Economics, the University of Michigan – Ann Arbor, Chuo University, and Korea University. He received a PhD from the University of Edinburgh and an MA from the University of Hawaii at Manoa. His major research interests include the various genres of business communication, the role of English as the business lingua franca, corporate communication in international contexts, and the pedagogical aspect of business communication.

Korean Business Communication

A Comprehensive Introduction

Yeonkwon Jung

Routledge
Taylor & Francis Group

LONDON AND NEW YORK

First published 2023
by Routledge
4 Park Square, Milton Park, Abingdon, Oxon OX14 4RN

and by Routledge
605 Third Avenue, New York, NY 10158

Routledge is an imprint of the Taylor & Francis Group, an Informa business

© 2023 Yeonkwon Jung

British Library Cataloguing-in-Publication Data
A catalogue record for this book is available from the British Library

ISBN: 978-0-367-62126-1 (hbk)
ISBN: 978-0-367-62125-4 (pbk)
ISBN: 978-1-003-10806-1 (ebk)

DOI: 10.4324/9781003108061

Typeset in Times New Roman
by Apex CoVantage, LLC

Contents

Acknowledgments

There were certain restrictions in conducting this research project during the COVID-19 pandemic. The joy of being able to complete this project is doubled in such a difficult situation. I would like to thank those helping me with this project.

I am indebted to Association for Business Communication (ABC). ABC's warm interest in my Korean business communication research became a major driving force in conducting this project. I take this opportunity to express my sincere appreciation to ABC.

I also owe many thanks to the Korean Association of English for Specific Purposes (ESP Korea). The appreciation plaque from ESP Korea was great encouragement to carry out this project.

Special thanks go to Prof. Hiromasa Tanaka (Meisei University) and Prof. Sky Marsen (Flinders University) for their insightful and constructive comments on this project. Surely, all errors are mine.

Last but not least, I would like to express my deepest gratitude to my lovely twin sisters, Yeonhee and Yeonhoe, and my two loves in Japan, Ryoko and Suzuka, for their moral support and endless love.

1 Introduction

1.1 Aim of the book

This book tries to demonstrate the heuristic value of the research on Korean business communication. It aims to conduct introductory but extensive work on Korean business communication in terms of putting stress on its situational aspect. It showcases research sharing the threefold denominator of *Korean* plus *business* plus *communication*. It deals with compound units rather than an individual unit among the denominator, such as Korean business, business communication, and Korean communication. Through this, it examines how business communication and Korean communication are projected onto Korean business. This process may enable us to address whether there is a continuum between Korean communication and business communication in Korea. On the other hand, it could be a measure of which of the three denominators, Korean, business, and communication, should be highlighted the most in cross-cultural business communication research such as this book. It could help us address if the East and West are indeed distinctive or overlapping. It seems important to address the question, as major Asian business communication research has a tendency to focus on cross-cultural communication involving Asian languages (together with English) in order to concentrate on the contrast between the East and West (e.g., Japanese [Miller 1994; Marriott 1997; Yamada 1997] and Chinese [Bilbow 1995, 1997; Rogerson-Revell 1998; Yeung 1998], to name a few). The application of conventional dichotomies is likely to fail to capture the complexities of differences among Asians. To overcome the weakness of Asian business communication research, recent studies on Asian business communication have sought to redefine cross-cultural business communication from the Asian perspective by examining the interaction between individuals of Asian backgrounds (e.g., Du-Babcock and Tanaka 2010; Paramasivam 2007). Given the claim of so-called postmodern Asian business communication research oriented to individual Asian cultural values,

DOI: 10.4324/9781003108061-1

this book adopts the local perspective of Korean business communication. It is an initial investigation into cultural values and their application to Korean business communication. Cultural values may significantly affect verbal and nonverbal business communication in Korea (see Chapter 4 for more detail). However, one may ask whether this view of culture is easily reconciled with the data from Korean business communication. This view may illustrate how much Korean culture plays a role in Korean business communication. Accordingly, this book determines proper cultural values within context. It introduces eclectic cases of Korean business communication situations, as communication patterns highly depend on the specific organizational context. Since the major aim of this book is not for investigating patterns of English as a lingua franca in intercultural business encounters but for exploring 'local' business communication in Korea, the language examined is monolingual, Korean. This book tries to address whether shared knowledge, such as national culture, is essential for communication success, even in local businesses. This approach may explain exceptions running counter to conventional or stereotypical cross-cultural communication knowledge, if indeed there are any. This book will be a useful reference to build intercultural communication studies on cultural values, as it is an academic effort to provide the audience knowledge far beyond cultural stereotypes in Korean business communication illustrated in some classical textbooks on Korean business communication (e.g., De Mente 2011, among many others).

1.2   Data in the book

Data in this book, specifically in reference to its three 'practical' chapters (i.e. Chapters 5, 6, and 7), are composed of Korean corporate communication data. Emphasis is given to passive or delayed interactive written exercises that range from the letter of a Korean business apology for complaint management, to a Korean CEO's online greetings to establish corporate credentials to stakeholders. Data also include a challenge or conflict element between or among interactants (e.g., complaint management in Korean service encounters).

Elsbach et al. (1998) argue that two sets of variables can be used to describe situations that need to be addressed by organizations. They explain that all events can be described on a continuum between anticipated and unanticipated and on a continuum between potentially positive and potentially negative. All exigencies facing organizations can be described as somewhere between fully anticipated and fully unanticipated. All exigencies facing organizations can also be described as having the potential to enhance or threaten perceptions of the organization. Together, these two sets of variables can help describe almost any rhetorical situation presented to an organization. Topics in the book are summarized with Elsbach et al.'s two sets of variables as follows:

1 Anticipated/positive:
   Empathy in a service encounter
   Nwunchi in a service encounter
   Senguy in a letter of apology
   Reason as accommodation statement in a letter of apology
   Volition in a CEO's online greeting
   Association with stakeholders in a CEO's online greeting
2 Anticipated/negative
   Politeness strategy in a service encounter
   Passive interaction in a letter of apology
   Reason as avoidance statement in a letter of apology
3 Unanticipated/positive
   Unmarked rudeness in intercultural business communication
4 Unanticipated/negative
   Lack of empathy in a service encounter
   Lack of *nwunchi* in a service encounter
   Kapcil in a service encounter
   Lack of *senguy* in a letter of apology
   Dissociation with stakeholders in a CEO's online greeting

In classical rhetoric, the canon of delivery was concerned with how a speaker used his voice and body to present and support the ideas of the speech. In those times, face-to-face speeches were the only outlet available for sharing ideas with public audiences. People who create communication for contemporary organizations can choose to deliver their messages through a wide range of print, broadcast, and internet outlets. It is important for a communicator to consider how organizational communicators disseminate their messages. Communicators should ask if the choice of outlet reinforces or contradicts the messages being sent (Hoffman and Ford 2010). In a similar vein, Gunnarsson (2009) also highlights the breadth and diversity of communicative interaction in workplace settings, emphasizing that

> [p]rofessional discourse can occur in different types of communicative events involving different constellations of participants: single person communicative events (individual writing and reading), two-person events (face to face interaction, written dialogues: letter exchange, e-mails, chat) and group events (small group meetings, written group correspondence, collaborative writing, collaborative presentations,

discussions, large group meetings, debates). It includes both communicative events in which all participants are in the same room as well as
communication at a distance, via telephone, internet, video, mail, etc.

(p. 7, emphasis is mine)

Besides face-to-face communication data, this book includes communication on the phone and call center communication to explore a vast spectrum
of communication channels.

1.3   Approach of the book

This book is the result of my academic journey to date. My major teaching
and research interests lie in the various genres of business communication,
the role of English as the business lingua franca in global business encounters, corporate communication in international contexts, and the pedagogical
aspect of teaching English business communication. The teaching experience exclusively at the College of International Professional Development,
Kansai Gaidai University (KGU), became a trigger for interest in the pedagogical aspect of teaching English business communication. Interest in its
pedagogical aspect became the motivation for conducting research on business communication curricula of communication departments in four-year
Korean universities at the School of Media and Communication, Korea University, for a year in 2016–2017. The research result becomes an important
ground for Chapter 3 of the book. It tries to address the question of whether
Korean business communicators *are* teaching business communication and,
if they are, which kinds of business communication they teach and which
traditions they follow. It defines the academic notion of Korean business
communication and illustrates how the definition links to research work on
teaching trends of Korean business communication in Korean higher education. After discussing cross-continental traditions of business communication (the American tradition of business communication and European
tradition of business communication), Chapter 2 discusses how those academic traditions affect research on Asian business communication locally
and globally. With the introduction to seminal research work on Asian business communication, such as Bargiela-Chiappini and Gotti (2005), *Journal of Asian Pacific Communication*'s special volume on Asian business
communication (parts 1 and 2), and Eastern Horizons: Enriching Business
Discourse Forum (Bargiela-Chiappini et al. 2007), it reviews the literature
on local Asian business communicators' research work, exclusively those
from Hong Kong, Japan, and the United Arab Emirates. Through analysis
of Asian business communication research trends in Chapter 2 and analysis
of Korean business communication curriculum in Korean higher education,

the current positioning of Korean business communication is considered in Chapter 3.

Research and education experience at various academic institutions across cultures helped me to form an interdisciplinary academic background. The interdisciplinary and diverse academic traces have a profound influence on the scope of my research on business communication and, naturally, the approach of this book. This book takes (verbal) linguistic competencies into consideration. Korean business communication data will be analyzed with the main sources of three types of competence: discourse competence (knowledge of genre), sociolinguistic competence (the ability to use language appropriately in different contexts, understanding readers, and adopting appropriate authorial attitudes), and strategic competence (the ability to use a variety of communicative strategies) (Canale and Swain 1980), for those chapters adopting practical perspective, Chapter 4 to Chapter 7.

1.3.1 Discourse competence

The work of seminal genre analysts (i.e., Swales 1990; Bhatia 1993) has tended to explicate language use through formal and functional aspects of discourse (e.g., move structure and intertextuality) in a *conventionalized* communicative setting. Swales (1990, 2002) defines genre based on communicative purposes. He describes genre as 'a class of communicative event' characterized by a set of communicative purposes. According to him, communicative purposes are highlighted as a fundamental feature that sets constraints for the stylistic and linguistic choices of genre. Communicative purposes as a fundamental feature in defining genres are relevant to the first step when planning communication (e.g., is the writer's message mainly to deliver objective information, is it mainly persuasive, or is it to create solidarity?). All messages have an underlying purpose. For example, the purpose of a credit refusal letter is to refuse the request while encouraging the customer's continued business. Creating goodwill is especially important when communicating unwelcome news with business partners. This book discusses genre-specific features of Korean business communication data. On the one hand, it investigates what makes the letter of Korean business apology passive in interaction. On the other hand, it supports the claim that a Korean CEO's online greeting genre is not prediction-oriented but volition-oriented. Besides, it discusses 'rhetoric as identity' in order to see how an organization determines its identity by illustrating its volition in CEO's online greeting genre. It also explicates a business organization's image management language highlighted in a Korean CEO's online greetings. It looks at the types of languages Korean CEOs use in the ways they do in the contemporary business world. It suggests a linguistic code of conduct that CEOs highlight when formulating online messages for stakeholders (e.g., corporate values, corporate social responsibility, sustainability). It aims to help stakeholders make sense of organizational behavior and words, which can be manipulated and shaped by corporate codes of conduct and guidelines for appropriate behavior in certain organizations (Jung 2012). It accommodates 'rhetoric as (nominalized) action' in order to identify language components Korean CEOs use to communicate with stakeholders (Eccles and Nohria 1992). It discusses how business communicators offer credibility in the PR communication genre. It suggests how Korean CEOs establish trust with the notion of Crichton's (2013) grounds for trust, such as calculus-based trust.

1.3.2   Sociolinguistic competence

The reference to genre analysis is not necessarily taking context into consideration. Until recently, genre studies in professional contexts have been on the use of 'text-internal linguistic resources' without an in-depth analysis of 'text-external sources', which are context (Bhatia 2012). Context should be incorporated exclusively in order to explain certain language use in goal-oriented business contexts. In other words, 'discourse as genre' is far beyond 'discourse as text', as its main concern lies in genre use *in* business practice. This book analyzes Korean business communication data in terms of using context to make inferences about meaning. That is, it investigates the products of communication, including the situatedness of language and its consequences and the particular language features seen as signaling contextual presuppositions or shared meanings, providing an interpretive framework for understanding business discourse. The same is true for approaches in pragmatics. Approaches in pragmatics go beyond *conventional* discourse analysis in that they draw on the context-sensitive position (Blum-Kulka 1997). Pragmatics adopting the context-sensitive position offers insights into cross-cultural communication (Blum-Kulka et al. 1989; Wierzbicka 1991). The value of this approach 'mediates the connection between language and social context and facilitates more satisfactory bridging of the gap between texts and contexts' (Fairclough 1995: 189) so that it allows us to reflect on 'who uses language, how, why and when' (Van Dijk 2011: 2). Words can mean more – or something other – than what they say. Their interpretation depends on a multiplicity of factors, including familiarity with the context and cultural assumptions. The same phrase may have different meanings on different occasions, and the same intention may be expressed by different linguistic means. The function or intention of each clause is contextually decided in this book (Connor et al. 1995; Upton and Connor 2001). Because utterances can simultaneously carry multiple meanings when they are taken out of context, the function of each unit is contextually determined. In this respect, pragmatic processes, such as speech acts and face theory, are adopted in the book to analyze how speakers seek to encode their messages for a particular audience and how speakers make inferences when seeking to locate a speaker's intended meaning. For example, this book explores the quality of attention to communication with people having great distance and power differences in Korean service encounters. It pays particular attention to the concept of *you*-attitude (communication perspective taking things from the other's perspective). Namely, it attempts to emphasize that the hearer's expectations need to be met for communicative success. It investigates the hearer's perspective of communicative behavior. It explores *senguy*, 'sincerity', as a device for meeting *you*-attitude requirements and investigates how *senguy* is realized in the letter of a Korean business apology. A discussion is also made on empathy in Korean service encounters. This book builds the foundation for empathy as emotional intelligence in Korean service encounters. It adopts Hogan's (1975) definition and classification of empathy communication, such as listening closely to customers (attentive empathy), offering emotional support (affective empathy), and anticipating needs (cognitive empathy). Despite the minor number of spoken data used in Chapter 5 (e.g., talk in sales encounters), conversation analysis is not used as a methodological tool as it has been criticized as too closely tied to Western interactional patterns and insensitive to cultural diversity (Gumperz 1982; Duranti 1988). Because of the limited previous or current work on Korean business communication, introductory work like this book inevitably adopts a synchronic approach. Translations of the Korean data are done into English with the greatest care, as they may remain a problem. Yale's romanization system is used to transcribe Korean into English.

1.3.3 Strategic competence

The term 'strategy' or 'strategic' is used to imply an intentional choice of how to proceed. Emphasis is given to communication strategies for politeness purposes. Politeness is of crucial importance to performing a goal-oriented activity, such as business. For example, politeness plays a crucial role in looking for a buyer, making the buyer respond favorably to sales letters or having the buyer purchase the product for sale. If a seller is not polite to a buyer, the buyer is unlikely to react in a favorable way to what the seller requests. Politeness may help both parties build trust and respect in order to maintain long-term business relationships. In this respect, it is seen as a necessary avenue for establishing a productive business atmosphere. In addition, it may serve the important function of handling negotiation processes and managing conflicts successfully. Therefore, politeness seems of vital importance in business settings to achieve a goal successfully. Major politeness scholars (Lakoff 1973; Leech 1983; Brown and Levinson 1987) have carried out research on the realization of politeness strategies in making face-threatening messages more implicit or less explicit. In this respect, over the last few decades, (in)directness has been one of the most popular cognitive values across cultures in studies on politeness. In particular, it has become a crucial (non)linguistic feature or convention for politeness. Since directness is characterized as intrinsically face-threatening or impolite, it is necessary to be indirect for politeness purposes (Brown and Levinson 1987). In other words, indirectness has been defined as a set of politeness strategies used to avoid or minimize imposition on the hearer and to create solidarity between interactants. The theoretical basis in Chapter 4 is Brown and Levinson's (1987) theory of politeness, one of the most well-known research studies on strategic politeness. Since face-threats are inherent properties of illocutionary acts, Brown and Levinson believe that it is necessary to study the threats to 'face wants' (see Chapter 4) in the context of speech acts. Therefore, more than others, Brown and Levinson's model explicitly provides how facework is reflected in politeness strategies used in the performance of speech acts. This book revisits Brown and Levinson's theory of politeness in Chapter 4. It argues whether an indirect message in a face-threatening situation is indeed indirect so that it is polite or, whether a face-threat is inherently impolite. Besides Brown and Levinson's work, I shall, where it is necessary, draw upon other approaches (e.g., Spencer-Oatey's theory of rapport management). Other approaches may, to some extent, explain those cases where Brown and Levinson's patterns of politeness strategy distribution are not consistent with or escape the data in the book.

1.4   Organization of the book

This book is composed of two parts: theory, and practice. First, the book provides an overview of theoretical aspects of Korean business communication. Chapter 2 reviews some selective Asian business communication studies. Alongside the major research trend of Asian business communication illustrated in Chapter 2, Chapter 3 investigates the contemporary academic trend of business communication in Korean higher education.

The rest of the chapters examine the practical aspects of Koreanb business communication from eclectic perspectives. Chapter 4 shows how Korean business professionals manage facework in business situations within the communication rules or cultural values. It addresses whether the value of indirectness is equally applicable to Korean business politeness.

Chapter 5 centers on the negative aspect of the interaction in Korean service encounters – that is, why service encounters might be perceived as unsuccessful. It focuses on issues of customer dissatisfaction (Gutek 1995; Gutek et al. 1999). It builds the foundation for empathy as emotional intelligence and adopts Hogan's (1975) definition and classification of empathy communication. It also induces two useful terms one may consider in Korean service encounters, *nwunchi*, or the ability to read another's face or feeling, and *kapcil*, or bossing around, as a kind of hallmark for success in customer relationship management in Korea.

As an extension of Chapter 5, Chapter 6 explicates the letter of a Korean business apology. The reciprocal nature of communication behaviors for making an apology is discussed using the notion of *senguy* (성의, 'sincerity').

Before concluding with implications for pedagogy and future research, Chapter 7 explicates prior orientation to work and priorities in what Korean companies want from their work. Sample Korean CEO's online greeting texts are chosen as major data of the chapter. It suggests that CEOs highlight a linguistic code of conduct when formulating online messages for stakeholders. It investigates whether the code is properly incorporated into a CEO's online public relations communication and whether companies put stress on specific codes of conduct.

References

Bargiela-Chiappini, F., Chakorn, O., Chew., G., Jung, Y., Kong, K.C.C., Nair-Venugopal, S., & Tanaka, H. (2007). Eastern Horizons: Enriching Business Discourse. *Discourse and Communication*, 1(2), 37–58.

Bargiela-Chiappini, F., & Gotti, M. (Eds.) (2005). *Asian Business Discourse(s)*. Bern: Peter Lang.

Bhatia, V. (1993). *Analysing Genre: Language Use in Professional Settings*. London: Longman.

Bhatia, V. (2012). Professional written genres. In J.P. Gee & M. Handford (Eds.) *The Routledge Handbook of Discourse Analysis* (pp. 239–251). London: Routledge.

Bilbow, G. (1995). Requesting strategies in the cross-cultural business meeting. *Pragmatics* 5(1), 45–55.

Bilbow, G. (1997). Spoken discourse in the multicultural workplace in Hong Kong: Applying a model of discourse as 'impression management'. In F. Bargiela-Chiappini & S. Harris (Eds.) *The Languages of Business: An International Perspective* (pp. 21–48). Edinburgh: Edinburgh University Press.

Blum-Kulka, S. (1997). Discourse pragmatics. In T.A. Van Dijk (Ed.) *Discourse as Structure and Process: Discourse Studies Vol. 2: A Multidisciplinary Introduction* (pp. 38–63). London: Sage.

Blum-Kulka, S., House, J., & Kasper, G. (1989). *Cross-Cultural Pragmatics: Requests and Apologies*. Ablex.

Brown, P., & Levinson, S. (1987). *Politeness: Some Universals in Language Use.* Cambridge: Cambridge University Press.

Canale, M., & Swain, M. (1980). Theoretical bases of communicative approaches to second language teaching and testing. *Applied Linguistics*, 1(1), 1–47.

Connor, U., Davis, K., & De Rycker, T. (1995). Correctness and clarity in applying for overseas jobs: A cross-cultural analysis of U.S. and Flemish applications. *Text*, 15(4), 457–476.

Crichton, J. (2013). 'Will there be flowers shoved at me?' a study in organizational trust, moral order and professional integrity. In C. Candlin & J. Crichton (Eds.) *Discourse of Trust* (pp. 119–132). Basingstoke: Palgrave Macmillan.

De Mente, B.L. (2011). *Korean Business Etiquette: The Cultural Values and Attitudes that Make Up the Korean Business Personality.* Tuttle Publishing.

Du-Babcock, B., & Tanaka, H. (2010). *Turn-taking behavior and topic management strategies of Chinese and Japanese business professionals: A comparison of intercultural group communication.* Association for Business Communication 2010 Annual Convention Proceedings.

Duranti, A. (1988). Communicative competence. In J. Mey (Ed.) *Concise Encyclopedia of Pragmatics.* Amsterdam: Pergamon.

Eccles, R.G., & Nohria, N. (1992). *Beyond the Hype: Rediscovering the Essence of Management.* Cambridge, MA: Harvard Business School Press.

Elsbach, K.D., Sutton, R.M., & Principe, K.E. (1998). Averting expected challenge through anticipatory impression management: A study of hospital billing. *Organization Science,* 9, 68–86.

Fairclough, N. (1995). *Critical Discourse Analysis: The Critical Study of Language.* London: Longman.

Gumperz, J. (1982). *Discourse Strategies:* Nev York: Cambridge University.

Gunnarsson, B-L. (2009). *Professional Discourse.* London: Bloomsbury.

Gutek, B.A. (1995). *The Dynamics of Service: Reflections on the Changing Nature of Customer/Provider Interaction.* San Francisco, CA: Jossey-Bass.

Gutek, B.A., Bhappu, A.D., Liao-Troth, M. A, & Cerry, B. (1999). Distinguishing between service relationships and encounters. *Journal of Applied Psychology*, 84(2), 218–233.

Hoffman, M., & Ford, P. (2010). *Organizational Rhetoric.* Thousand Oaks: Sage publications.

Hogan, R. (1975). Empathy: A conceptual and psychometric analysis. *The Counselling Psychologist*, 5(2), 14–18.

Jung, Y. (2012). Work orientation in Korean CEO's on-line greetings. *Online Journal of Communication and Media Technologies*, 2(2), 153–181.

Lakoff, R. (1973). *The logic of politeness: Or minding your p's and q's.* Proceedings of the Ninth Regional Meeting of the Chicago Linguistic Society, 292–305.

Leech, G. (1983). *Principles of Pragmatics.* London: Longman.

Marriott, H. (1997). Australian-Japanese business interaction: Some features of language and cultural contact. In F. Bargiela-Chiappini & S. Harris (Eds.) *The Languages of Business: An International Perspective* (pp. 49–71). Edinburgh: Edinburgh University Press.

Miller, L. (1994). Japanese and American indirectness. *Journal of Asian Pacific Communication*, 5(1–2), 1–19.

Paramasivam, S. (2007). A discourse-oriented model for analysing power and politeness in negotiation interaction: A cross-linguistic perspective. *Journal of Universal Language*, 8, 91–127.

Rogerson-Revell, P. (1998). *Interactive style and power at work: An analysis of discourse in intercultural business meetings*. Unpublished PhD Thesis. University of Birmingham.

Swales, J.M. (1990). *Genre Analysis: English in Academic and Research Settings*. Cambridge: Cambridge University Press.

Swales, J.M. (2002). On models of applied discourse analysis. In C. Candlin (Ed.) *Research and Practice in Professional Discourse* (pp. 61–77). Hong Kong: City University of Hong Kong Press.

Upton, T., & Connor, U. (2001). Using computerized corpus analysis to investigate the textlinguistic discourse moves of a genre. *English for Specific Purposes*, 20(4), 313–329.

Van Dijk, T. (2011). *Discourse Studies: A Multidisciplinary Introduction* (2nd ed.) London: Sage

Wierzbicka, A. (1991). *Cross-Cultural Pragmatics: The Semantics of Social Interaction*. Mouton de Gruyter.

Yamada, H. (1997). *Different Games, Different Rules: Why Americans and Japanese Misunderstand Each Other*. Oxford: Oxford University Press.

Yeung, L. (1998). Linguistic forms of consultative management discourse. *Discourse and Society*, 9(1), 81–101.

2 Asian business communication

2.1 Initiation of the Asian business communication project

Business communication, which was a largely Western-centered study, began relatively late in Asia. The driving force for business communication centered on Asia was Dr. Francesca Bargiela-Chiappini, now retired. As a permanent research professor at the University of Trent University in Nottingham, UK, she recognized the importance of Asian business communication and, in 2003, launched an Asian Business Discourse(s) project with Asian business communication major scholars. The discussions of the project teams resulted in various kinds of publications. First, for example, there is a book titled *Asian Business Discourse(s)* (Peter Lang Publishing House), published and edited in 2005 by Bargiela-Chiappini and Gotti. The book reflects the vigorous interest in studies of business discourse(s) and culture(s) emerging from various Asian communities. It also records the diversity of methodological approaches, ontological perspectives, and topics characterizing a number of studies conducted by Asian and Western scholars on cultural and linguistic strategies and preferences identifiable in Asian or Asian-Western business interactions. The volume is structured in two parts, including chapters that address linguistic and textual issues (part 1) and cultural and pragmatic issues (part 2) of Asian business discourse(s). Second, there is a special issue on Asian business communication (parts 1 and 2) of the *Journal of Asian Pacific Communication*. In the first volume of the *Asia Pacific Communication Journal*, volume 15, number 2 (2005), the concept of Asian business communication, the necessity of the study, and the challenges facing cross-cultural communication research in business communication are considered from an Asian perspective. The subsequent volume (volume 16, number 1 [2006]) discusses business meetings that use English as a lingua franca along with Asian languages (e.g., Japanese, Malay, Thai, Chinese). Publication projects under the rubric of 'Asian

DOI: 10.4324/9781003108061-2

Business Discourse(s)' (Bargiela-Chiappini 2005, 2006; Bargiela-Chiappini and Gotti 2005) brought to the attention of the international readership an original body of research on discursive business practices and organizational communication issues in a variety of Asian cultures. Finally, in the forum Eastern Horizons: Enriching Business Discourse (Bargiela-Chiappini et al. 2007a), Bargiela-Chiappini and her colleagues, who represented numerous Asian countries, discuss some of the topics highlighted by the project, frequently focusing on subjects that arise from recent indigenous research in business discourse as a multidisciplinary field. The forum tries to provide a window into a non-Western perspective within communication research in business settings and reflect on some of the salient topics that occupy researchers involved in the analysis, interpretation, and improvement of communication practices in the workplace. Selective topics in the forum include the concept of culture, the function of politeness, the importance of organizational face, the role of indirectness and of personal orientation in both written and spoken communication, and the interplay of power, politeness, and solidarity in business in-groups, among others. The majority of the work of Asian business communication researchers appeared in the Linguistics Insights Series, and the *Journal of Asian Pacific Communication* (Bargiela-Chiappini and Gotti 2005; Bargiela-Chiappini 2005; Bargiela-Chiappini 2006), both of which adopt the European tradition of business communication. The following section introduces some notable research work on Asian business communication in conjunction with the characteristics of the European tradition of business communication.

2.2 Asian business communication research from a European perspective

Business communication research in the European tradition has generally been the preserve of applied linguists, many of whom come from the world of English for specific business purposes (ESBP) (Nickerson and Planken 2009). It has been contextual in its approach. Contextual language use is a hallmark of the English for specific purposes (ESP) and language for specific purposes (LSP) field in general and of professional genre analysis, and this influence has been apparent in much of the work carried out. European researchers have frequently investigated the relationship between contextual variables (Chalres 1996; Nickerson 2000). They have paid special attention to the use of English as a lingua franca (ELF) in international business (e.g., Firth 1996; Nickerson 2000; Poncini 2004; Planken 2005; Rogerson-Revell 2007; Bargiela-Chiappini et al. 2007b; Louhiala-Salminen et al. 2005; Seidlhofer 2004). For example, Louhiala-Salminen et al. (2005) studied ELF encounters within the context of business mergers and introduced the concept of BELF (business ELF, or English as a business lingua franca) to refer to the language that business professionals from different cultural and linguistic and linguistic backgrounds use to conduct their daily work activities. They applied the concept of BELF to emphasize the overall communicative goal and the domain of use of ELF. According to Louhiala-Salminen et al. (2005), BELF speakers share the 'B', or the context and knowledge of business, and the 'E', or at least the 'core', of the English language and, to some extent, its discourse practices. However, they are, at the same time, separated by the previous knowledge and experience connected with their various native languages and related discourse practices and their own, often hidden and implicit rules of communication. The BELF perspective is aimed at drawing attention to the central role that the language of communication plays in interaction. By emphasizing the distinction between English and ELF/BELF, they also want to question the validity of the straightforward association between English and, consequently, the discursive norms of English. Given the claim, some Asian business communicators also work on the use of ELF in business contexts. For instance, the ELF project – titled Industry-University ELF English as a Common Language) Usage Survey and Recommendations for Global Human Resource Development English Education (2014–2019) – led by Kumiko Murata at Waseda University investigates the actual use of ELF in both academic and business contexts in Japan or in the context which includes Japanese users of ELF. In so doing, the project employs discourse and pragmatic perspectives for its analyses of recorded data which are collected while researchers observe ELF interactions. They use participants' interviews and questionnaires on the use of ELF. An ethnographic approach of participant observation and interviews, paying special attention to what is going on in its actual use with its resultant effects and problems, is adopted. On the basis of detailed descriptions of what is really happening in these interactions, the project ultimately intends to contribute a better understanding of ELF use in actual situations and to the planning of or reconsideration for educational policies or curriculum and/or syllabus designs that accommodate the need for ELF users in both academic and business contexts. It is to suggest some practical implications for language teaching to develop ELF competencies/ capabilities. Du-Babcock and Tanaka (2016) investigate leadership in a setting where ELF is used among Asian business professionals. Employing the notion of discourse, they use quantitative and qualitative analyses to identify how leadership emerges in meetings with multicultural participants and how different types of leadership affect these decision-making meetings. They conclude that linguistic and contextual factors discursively construct different styles of leadership and that these leadership styles lead to starkly different team outcomes. They indicate that a business meeting is not a logical process leading to a rational decision but rather an organic mix of contextual, linguistic, and leadership factors when ELF is used in multicultural participants. Nickerson and Camiciottoli (2013) present the results of a survey of the attitudes of Emirati consumers toward the use of English in advertising texts in the United Arab Emirates (UAE). They discuss the survey findings in terms of the unique social and cultural fabric of the modern-day UAE, as well as of the Emirati community as an economically powerful Muslim population. Nickerson (2015) asks how we can best focus our research efforts and then design our teaching language for specific business purposes in the Asia Pacific region and the Middle East. In parts 1 and 2 of the article, she discusses how we need to (1) refer to empirical evidence as the basis for our teaching and training materials, (2) become more aware of the challenges posed by globalization, (3) understand the role played for business people by ELF, alongside other languages, and (4) develop closer ties with people working in business and industry. In part 3, she discusses (1) a teaching project involving undergraduate research that is a course for her senior business students on workplace communication and (2) the development of an evaluation instrument to chart her students' progress in terms not only of their language proficiency but also their communication knowledge and skills.

Although English has been a dominating influence, as in other research traditions around the world, the European tradition has also included the investigation of European languages other than English. Although English has been a dominating presence in much European work, many other European languages have also been investigated, such as French (Van der Wijst 1996), Dutch (Van der Wijst 1996), German (Zilles 2004), Spanish (Villemoes 2003; Conaway and Wardrope 2004), Danish (Grindsted 1997), Norwegian (Neumann 1997), and Portuguese (Silvestein 2003). Some Asian business communicators also adopt this local perspective. For example, Tanaka (2011) examines the Japanese data collected during an intra-organizational meeting in a Japanese company. It illustrates how, in a situation involving potential conflicts, some Japanese managers switch between different linguistic codes in order to construct situational meaning. He claims that the interlocutors' code-switching indicates constant vertical and horizontal changes of their footing by sometimes strengthening solidarity with subordinates and mitigating potential face-threatening acts (FTAs). He indicates that the use of honorifics and other social indexical forms in Japanese is not pre-determined by existing social conventions, but rather, it is subject to situational evaluation of the fluid local context where relationships are constructed and negotiated. Fujio and Tanaka (2012) attempt to apply an epistemological framework based on concepts developed by business discourse scholars. They seek to bridge the gap between Japanese discourse analysis and the study of organizations in Japan by setting the analysis of the Japanese business meeting data. Nickerson and Goby (2017) examine ways to counteract the arbitrary mix of organizational communication practices that have evolved in the Gulf region as a result of the large numbers of different cultures that make up the workforce there. They attempt to develop a conceptual model of leadership communication, the Gulf Leadership Communication Framework, a crucial element in organizational communication practices that is of particular relevance for the process of localization in the Gulf region. In this analysis, they refer to two sets of empirical data on discursive leadership and interpersonal communication that were collected from around 600 Emirati nationals. Their findings show that a leadership model for social contexts, like the Gulf Cooperation Council, may look very different from the models that obtain elsewhere. Goby and Nickerson (2016) identify the rudiments of an organizational communication framework that can serve as a facilitator of a positive diversity climate, which could enhance the integration of locals into the expatriate-dominated workforce of the UAE. The study elicits 458 Emirati respondents' narratives of positive and negative workplace communication experiences. The authors identify emerging themes to highlight the key features of interpersonal interactions likely to foster or hinder a supportive diversity climate. They interpret data in terms of UAE cultural traditions – more specifically, the communication patterns valued by local workers. They attempt to reestablish a preference for indigenous communication practices to facilitate the workforce localization policies that are present in many Gulf countries. Goby and Nickerson (2016) conducted a preliminary investigation of how locals are responding to the growing number of CSR initiatives that are being implemented in the United Arab Emirates. Moreover, given that scholars have argued that Islamic principles of philanthropy should guide CSR initiatives in Muslim countries, they also consider if their Emirati respondents connect CSR with Islamic philanthropy. Results from their survey of 267 local Muslim consumers in Dubai indicate that CSR is not typically equated with philanthropy. In addition, respondents displayed an appreciation of the economic benefits that CSR can generate. Their research implies that organizations in Dubai no longer need to base their CSR on the platform of Islamic philanthropy, as many scholars have argued. They suggest that in wealthy emerging nations, CSR may not be predominantly interpreted as corporate philanthropy, which is needed in poorer developing economies for the provision of infrastructure, schools, hospitals, and housing, and which in some Muslim contexts is also implemented because of local religious values.

The local perspective illustrated above becomes a solid groundwork for cross-cultural business communication research in Asia. Seminal research work on cross-cultural communication by Hofstede (2001) and Hall (1976) provides a framework for cultural differences in Asian business communication. Hofstede's study of cultural dimensions identifies Western countries as individualist and Asian countries as collectivist. Hall differentiates high-context and low-context communication styles, with high-context communication predominating in Asian countries and low-context communication predominating in Western countries. These research paradigms provide the basis for research studies on the impact of cultures on (non)verbal behaviors in inter-Asian business encounters. Yamada (1997) brings an insider perspective and a linguist training to the question, illuminating the many reasons that Americans and the Japanese misunderstand one another. She explains that social organization shapes the way we converse. Because American and Japanese cultures value different kinds of social relationships, they play different language games with different sets of rules. She outlines the basic differences between Japanese and American English and analyzes a number of real-life business and social interactions in which these differences led to miscommunication. She suggests, for instance, that US meetings and Japanese meetings emerge from, and respond to, different goals. In the United States, meetings are a response to the need to manage the business tasks at hand, and the goal is decision-making. By contrast, meetings in Japan respond to the need for an effective exchange of opinions, and the goal is to manage the ongoing relationship between colleagues. These different goals influence vocabulary and grammar selection in context. Namely, Japanese meetings begin at the time of 'shouting goals' to establish the cohesiveness of the group and to confirm the favor between business members. In US meetings, the work goals of the meetings are completed first; only when the 'business' concludes do interpersonal relationships form. Fujio (2004) seeks to deconstruct business stereotypes by examining meeting data of Japanese and US employees. She finds that Japanese participants do not necessarily follow the indirect communication style. Murata (2014) fills a gap in empirical cross-cultural studies, drawing on authentic Japanese workplace discourse. She reports a qualitative analysis of humor in Japanese and New Zealand business meetings, describing its manifestations and functions. She indicates that (1) though humor serves as a relational practice, its manifestations are distinctive in each community of practice (CofP), and (2) meeting members enact relational practice through humor in ways that meet the underlying expectations of each CofP. Du-Babcock and Tanaka (2013) compare the communication behaviors of business professionals from two prominent Asian cultures – Japanese culture, and Hong Kong Chinese culture – when these professionals participate in intercultural and intracultural decision-making meetings. The study reveals some differences in communication behaviors between the two cultural groups in both the intracultural and the intercultural meetings. Although both groups generally reflect their high-context communication orientations, they exhibit some deviations from the general discourse patterns, especially in the ways in which they expressed disagreements. Cheng and Lam (2013) study the Western perceptions of and relations with Hong Kong a decade after the reversion of the sovereignty from Britain to China in 1997. They investigate the West's understanding, opinions, and positions regarding Hong Kong today compared with those in 1997. The possible reasons for any changes are also investigated. They examine a range of Western public discourses regarding Hong Kong concerning the handover. They yield insights into the new Hong Kong in the eyes of the West, which in turn contributes to a reexamination of the relations and power balance between the West and China.

It has been largely neutral in its approach to the analysis of European business discourse has been neutral in its analysis – that is, it has not sought to identify or redress any existing hegemonies in the European business world as evidenced in its discourse. European researchers have pursued a descriptive, mostly neutral set of objectives. The intention has been to describe what is happening in the business interaction or document, perhaps to design a better language training course or a more effective document (Marschan-Piekkari et al. 2005). As an application of the European tradition to Asian business communication, for instance, Lockwood (2012) investigates how current applied linguistic research into the nature of call center communication breakdown in business processing outsourcing (BPO) sites, such as India and the Philippines, can impact English communications training program content and design for this industry. She argues that a research-based approach to English for specific purposes (ESP) syllabus design and content will yield improved outcomes. She focuses on the interface between the research and the design and content rather than the implementation and evaluation of the program. She uses a case study of an ESP curriculum development project commissioned by a large multinational company operating global call centers and back offices in Asia for the investigation. Her article outlines the theoretical principles upon which this ESP syllabus was developed and then traces the steps in integrating the findings and tailoring the program to the needs of this multinational worksite. Hood and Forey (2008) investigate how speakers contribute to the interactive rise and fall of emotion in problematic interactions in a data set of inbound telephone conversations collected from call centers in the Philippines. These interactions are between Filipino customer service representatives (CSR) and American clients who initiate the calls to seek information, clarification, or resolution to a problem. Their study draws on appraisal theory to analyze the contribution of the caller and the CSR to initiating, maintaining, and adjusting the interpersonal intensity of the interaction. They point to a limited reliance on explicit attitude on the part of both speakers, with an attitude more often implied rather than expressed explicitly. Du-Babcock and Tanaka (2010) report the preliminary results of a study that extends Du-Babcock's turn-taking and topic management studies by examining the topic management strategies and turn-taking behaviors of bilingual Hong Kong Chinese and Japanese business professionals. This study is based on both quantitative and qualitative data. The quantitative data examine the differences between Hong Kong Chinese and Japanese business professionals in terms of their turn-taking, speaking time, and the number of words spoken. The qualitative data further examine the similarities and differences in their intercultural interaction. The preliminary findings show that there are differences between Japanese and Hong Kong business professionals in terms of their turn-taking behaviors (number of turns, amount of speaking time, and number of words) and topic management strategies (socializing, disclosure of opinions, hedging, and disagreement). In turn-taking, the Hong Kong Chinese participate more actively than Japanese business professionals in terms of the number of turns taken, amount of speaking time, and number of words spoken. In topic management strategies, the Hong Kong Chinese and Japanese exhibited similarities and differences. The socialization patterns (greetings and introductions) are similar. Differences exist in expressing opinions and disagreements. In expressing opinions, the Hong Kong Chinese exhibit an assertive behavior pattern, while the Japanese show reactive communication behavior. Disagreements are also expressed differently. The Hong Kong Chinese express disagreement directly, while the Japanese use hedging to express their disagreements. Bargiela-Chiappini and Tanaka (2011) reveal that the turn-taking frequency of managers are higher than that of employees when the discussion focuses on management issues. They conclude with the claim that the turn-taking frequency for employees and managers is equivalent when the discussion concerns employees' responsibilities, whereas the unequal distribution of turns may have arisen from participants' concern for relationship maintenance.

European business communication has usually involved some form of close text analysis and has often focused on authentic written texts or spoken events. European researchers have based their work on empirical data, whether in the form of sets of survey data based on written questionnaires and interviews, video recordings of meetings that took place in BELF, or emails written in BELF (Louhiala-Salminen et al. 2005; Planken 2005). Research on Asian business communication using corpus is remarkable. Cheng et al. (2005) describe a new addition to the growing number of spoken corpora, the Hong Kong Corpus of Spoken English (prosodic), which has the relatively rare and additional benefit of being both orthographically and prosodically transcribed. The corpus comprises approximately one million words spread evenly across four sub-corpora: academic discourses, business discourses, conversations, and public discourses. The corpus consists of over half of the full Hong Kong Corpus of Spoken English (orthographic), which is a two-million-word corpus of naturally occurring talk between Hong Kong Chinese and speakers of languages other than Cantonese. They describe the contents of the HKCSE (prosodic), the discourse intonation systems used to denote speakers' intonation choices, and the software specifically designed and implemented to interrogate the corpus, together with examples of some of the search functions available to the user. Cheng (2007) examines the use of vague language (VL) across different spoken genres in intercultural contexts. She analyzes representative samples of the academic, business, conversational, and public subcorpora in the Hong Kong Corpus of Spoken English (HKCSE), which is made up of Hong Kong Chinese and primarily native English speakers. She tries to find out how the use of VL compares across spoken genres and between the two sets of speakers. Cheng (2006) examines a selection of spoken discourse events collected in Hong Kong during and in the immediate aftermath of the SARS crisis in 2003. These discourse events form part of the HKCSE. The findings show that once the overlapping patterns of co-selection of the most frequently occurring lexical words in the SARS corpus have been determined, it is possible to describe the cumulative effects of the habitual co-selection in the lexical items that contribute to textual meanings and coherence within and across the texts. She argues that patterns of co-selection provide a fuller picture of textual and intertextual coherence than concentrating solely on lexical cohesion.

This chapter discusses some Asian business communication research influenced by the European tradition of business communication. Much literature on Asian business communication reviewed here is from scholars settled in East Asian countries, China (Hong Kong, in particular), and Japan, excluding Korea. The next chapter explores trends in business communication research and teaching in Korean higher education in order to exemplify the reason for the lack of academic popularity, which makes it difficult to keep track of previous work or major transitions in Korean business communication.

References

Bargiela-Chiappini, F. (Ed.) (2005/06) Double special issue on 'Asian Business Discourse(s)', *Journal of Asian Pacific Communication*.

Bargiela-Chiappini, F., & Gotti, M. (Eds.) (2005) *Asian Business Discourse(s)*. Bern: Peter Lang.

Bargiela-Chiappini, F., & Tanaka, H. (2011) The mutual gaze. Japan, management training and the west. In S. Nair-Venugopal (Ed.) *The Gaze of the West: Framings of the East* (pp. 139–155). London: Equinox.

Bargiela-Chiappini, F., Chakorn, O., Chew., G., Jung, Y., Kong, K.C.C., Nair-Venu-gopal, S., & Tanaka, H. (2007a). Eastern Horizons: Enriching Business Discourse. *Discourse and Communication*, 1(2), 37–58.

Bargiela-Chiappini, F., Nickerson, C. & Planken, B. (2007b). *Business Discourse*. Basingstoke: Palgrave Macmillan.

Charles, M. (1996). Business negotiations: Interdependence between discourse and the business relationship. *English for Specific Purposes*, 15(1), 19–36.

Cheng, W. (2006). Describing the extended meanings of lexical cohesion in a corpus of SARS spoken discourse. *International journal of corpus linguistics*, 325–344.

Cheng, W. (2007). The use of vague language across spoken genres in an intercultural Hong Kong corpus. In J. Cutting (Ed.) *Vague Language Explored* (pp. 161–181). Palgrave Macmillan.

Cheng, W., & Lam, P. (2013). Western perceptions of Hong Kong ten years on: A Corpus-driven critical discourse study applied linguistics. 34(2), 173–190.

Cheng, W., Greaves, C., & Warren, M. (2005). The creation of a prosodically transcribed intercultural corpus: The Hong Kong Corpus of Spoken English (prosodic). *ICAME Journal*, 47–68.

Conaway, R., & W. Wardrope. (2004). Communication in Latin America: An analysis of Guatemala business letters. *Business Communication Quarterly*, 67(4), 465–74.

Du-Babcock, B., & Tanaka, H. (2010). *Turn-taking behavior and topic management strategies of Chinese and Japanese business professionals: A comparison of intercultural group communication*. Proceedings of the 75th Annual Convention of the Association for Business Communication.

Du-Babcock, B., & Tanaka, H. (2013). A comparison of the communication behaviors of Hong Kong Chinese and Japanese business professionals in intracultural and intercultural decision-making meetings. *Journal of Business and Technical Communication*, 27(3), 263–287.

Du-Babcock, B., & Tanaka, H. (2016). Leadership construction in intra-Asian English as lingua franca decision-making meetings. *International Journal of Business Communication*, 54(1), 83–98.

Firth, A. (1996). The discursive accomplishment of normality. On 'lingua franca' English and conversation analysis. *Journal of Pragmatics*, 26, 237–259.

Fujio, M. (2004). Silence during intercultural communication: A case study. *Corporate Communication*, 94, 331–39.

Fujio, M., & Tanaka, H. (2012). 'Harmonious disagreement' in Japanese business discourse. In Y. Aritz & R. Walker (Eds.) *Discourse Perspectives in Organizational Communication* Madison: Dickinson University Press.

Goby, V.P., & Nickerson, C. (2016). Conceptualization of CSR among Muslim consumers in Dubai: Evolving from philanthropy to ethical and economic orientations. *Journal of Business Ethics*. 136, 167–179.

Goby V.P., Nickerson, C., & David, E. (2015). Interpersonal communication and diversity climate: promoting workforce localization in the UAE. *International Journal of Organizational Analysis*, 23(3), 364–377.

Grindsted, A. (1997). Joking as a strategy in Spanish and Danish negotiations. In F. Bargiela-Chiappini & S. Harris (Eds.) *The Languages of Business: An International Perspective* (pp. 159–82). Edinburgh: Edinburgh University Press.

Hall, E.T. (1976). *Beyond culture.* N.Y.: Doubleday.

Hofstede, G. (2001). *Cultures and Organizations* (2nd ed.). London: HarperCollinsBusiness.

Hood, S., & Forey, G. (2008). The interpersonal dynamics of call-centre interactions: Co-constructing the rise and fall of emotion. *Discourse and Communication*, 2(4), 389–409

Lockwood, J. (2012). Developing an English for specific purpose curriculum for Asian call centres: How theory can inform practice. *English for Specific Purposes*, 31, 14–24.

Louhiala-Salminen, L., Charles, M., & Kankaanranta, A. (2005). English as a lingua franca in Nordic corporate mergers. Two case companies. *English for Specific Purposes*, 24(4), 401–21.

Marschan-Piekkari, R.E., Vaara, J. Tienari, & Santti, R. (2005). Integration or disintegration? Human resource implications of the common corporate language decision in a cross-border merger. *International Journal of Human Resource Management*, 16(3), 333–47.

Murata, K. (2014). An empirical cross-cultural study of humour in business meetings in New Zealand and Japan. *Journal of Pragmatics*, 60, 251–265.

Neumann, I. (1997). Requests in German-Norwegian business discourse: Differences in directness. In F. Bargiela-Chiappini & S. Harris (Eds.) *The Languages of Business: An International Perspective* (pp. 72–73). Edinburgh: Edinburgh University Press.

Nickerson, C. (2000). *Playing the Corporate Language Genre: An Investigation of the Genres and Discourse Strategies in English used by Dutch Writers Working in Multinational Corporations*. Amsterdam: Rodopi.

Nickerson, C. (2015). Unity in diversity: The view from the (UAE) classroom. *Language Teaching*, 48(2), 235–249.

Nickerson, C., & Camiciottoli, B.C. (2013). Business English as a lingua franca in advertising texts in the Arabian Gulf: Analyzing the attitudes of the emirati community. *Journal of Business and Technical Communication*, 27(3), 329–352.

Nickerson, C., & Goby, N.P.C. (2017). New lamps for old: The gulf leadership communication framework. *International Journal of Business Communication*, 54(2), 182–198.

Nickerson, C., & Planken, B. 2009. Europe: The state of the field. In F. Bargiela-Chiappini (Ed.) *The Handbook of Business Discourse* (pp. 18–29). Edinburgh: Edinburgh University Press.

Planken, B. (2005). Managing rapport in lingua franca sales negotiations: A comparison of professional and aspiring negotiators. *English for Specific Purposes*, 24(4), 381–400.

Poncini, G. (2004). *Discourse Strategies in Multicultural Business Meetings*. Bern: Peter Lang.

Rogerson-Revell, P. (2007). Using English for international business: A European case study. *English for Specific Purposes*, 26, 103–20.

Seidlhofer, B. (2004). Research perspectives on teaching English as a lingua franca. *Annual Review of Applied Linguistics*, 24, 209–39.

Silvestein, M.C.B. (2003). *Continuities and changes in gender relations in the entrepreneurial discourse: From representations to leadership practice. A critical discourse analysis.* PhD thesis. University of Lisbon.

Tanaka, H. (2011). Politeness in a Japanese intra-organisational meeting: Honorifics and socio-dialectal code switching. *Journal of Asian Pacific Communication*, 21(1), 60–76.

Van der Wijst, P. (1996). *Politeness in requests and negotiations.* Ph.D. Dissertation. Katholieke Universiteit Brabant.

Villemoes, A. (2003). How do southern Spaniards create the conditions necessary to initiate negotiations with strangers? *Journal of Linguistics*, 31, 119–34.

Yamada, H. (1997). *Different Games, Different Rules.* New York: Oxford University Press.

Zilles, S. (2004). *Offers in German and Irish English business negotiations: A cross-cultural empirical analysis of micropragmatic and macropragmatic aspects.* Paper presented at the ABC European Conference, University of Milan.

3 Business communication in Korean higher education

3.1 Motivation to conduct the research

My curiosity about trends in Korean business communication research goes back 20 years from the present. First as a PhD student, and subsequently as a junior researcher in business communications, I was fully motivated to join a variety of conferences hosted by the Association for Business Communication (Jung 2001a, b, c, d; 2002; 2004; 2005a, b, c; among others) and to actively network with business communication scholars around the world. Among the many scholars, it was very rare to happen to meet up with Korean scholars working on business communication, and it was also difficult to see cases in which non-Korean business communication scholars conducted research on Korean business communication. Meanwhile, one global project motivated me to conduct research on the local situation of Korean business communication research. Dr. Francesca Bargiela-Chiappini, formerly a research professor at Nottingham Trent University, invited me to participate in writing *The Handbook of Business Discourse*, to be published by Edinburgh University Press (Bargiela-Chiappini (ed.) 2009). Although each chapter of the handbook was required to pay particular attention to its literature review due to the fundamental nature of the handbook, I faced difficulties in writing my chapter, about the so-called Korean business communication, due to a lack of prior research on the subject. The lack of prior research related to Korean business communication is still evident even in the related latest research. For instance, Du-Babcock (2018) conducts broad research on trends in business communication in Asia. She attempts to provide a plentiful literature review of business communication in Asia (East Asian countries, in particular) over the last two decades. She claims that Korean business practices, customs, and management systems are deeply influenced by cultural values. Her claim goes well along with Jung's (2009b) major findings on Korean business communication. Jung investigates cultural values and their application to Korean business

DOI: 10.4324/9781003108061-3

communication. For example, the nature of the hierarchical order is the underlying cause of the predominantly vertical nature of the relationships in Korean business organizations. Koreans are sensitive to indirectness. They tend to avoid openly expressing their opinions or feelings, even in business contexts. The collectivistic nature of Korean society causes strong family ties to be extended to the work environment so that the work organization can function very much like a family. This collective nature creates an effect on Korean management practices. A few *kulup* (a group of affiliated companies) owned by *chaebols* (conglomerates) advocate the *inhwa* style of management (e.g., LG Electronics). *Inhwa* ('human harmony') is a concept that incorporates both loyalty on the part of employees and maternal concern and behavior on the part of employers toward their workers. Although Du-Babcock's major arguments are marginally made on the Korean management system influenced by the Korean culture, the review of literature on Korean business communication research is not made in her research work, probably due to the reason for lack of prior research concerned, as indicated in Jung (2009b). The absence of relevant prevalent studies made local situation analysis more urgent. This short chapter aims to look into trends in business communication teaching in Korea to meet this academic demand based on the review of the major findings of the latest two research works concerned.

3.2 Trends of business communication teaching in Korean higher education

Two pieces of seminal research on the trend of business communication teaching in Korean higher education, Chang et al. (2018) and Jung (2018), are the recognition of the urgent need to grasp the awareness of Korean business communication in Korea. Chang et al. (2018) conducted research on the current state of business communication courses in the business schools of the top 30 Korean universities. Based on his research project conducted at the School of Media and Communication, Korea University, under the financial support of C.R. Anderson Research Funds (www.businesscommunication.org/page/anderson), Jung (2018) examines web content on business communication curricula of communication departments in four-year Korean universities and then conducts a content analysis of the websites of Korean communication associations, as well as related qualitative interviews with professors whose academic interest is related to business communication. Both articles were contributed to the inaugural 'English' journal of the Korean Association for Business Communication (KABC; www.kabc.re.kr). The demand for Korean business communication research became an opportunity for the birth of a new Korean academic association.

Its representative runner is KABC. KABC initiated to play a crucial role in being the prime platform for coordinating and increasing the awareness of Korean business communication locally and globally, as Watson (2019) duly noted its contribution. To activate Korean business communication research both domestically and internationally, KABC signed an MOU with advanced related academic associations (e.g., Association for Business Communication and Japan Association for Business Communication) and formed a multinational editorial board for its English journal, *Business Communication Research and Practice*. Chang et al. (2018) and Jung (2018) suggest some possible next steps that Korean business communication teachers can take for pedagogical purposes. Chang et al. (2018) try to provide a fundamental basis for curriculum development. They analyze department curricula and course syllabuses in order to see teaching (not researching) trend on business communication in Korea. They divide the course into three types of business communication courses: (1) business practice, focusing on the improvement of communication skills, the role of communication in organizations, strategic communication, and intercultural communication for a globalized society; (2) technical skills, focusing on preparing students for interviews, English resumes and cover letters, business document writing, presentations, and marketing oneself; and (3) specialized functions, focusing on specific functions of business such as developing skills such as negotiation, marketing, and CSR. Based on the analysis of the three types of business communication courses from the quantitative approach, they found that the three types in Korea had almost balanced weights. Despite clear-cut categorization into three types up to the 'official' title of each course, there seems to be a certain limitation to see whether each instructor teaches the particular topic, as it is. Knight (1999) recognizes that contradictory information may often appear throughout a particular website because some websites serve primarily not as resources for specific information but as marketing tools. Chang et al. (2018) also recognized the pitfall of web research. That is, in Korea, although most university business departments offer communication courses, the content and style of a particular business communication course usually depend on what the instructor wishes to teach, which leads to a variety of syllabuses for different courses with a shared name. In this respect, it is a bit problematic to quantify business communication courses in Korean higher education with web research. In order to implement this limitation, Jung's (2018) study more like focuses on the perception of business communication itself using Miller's (1996) categorization of business communication with some revisions (i.e., managerial communication, organizational communication, corporate communication, intercultural communication, and professional communication). Namely, he investigates the contemporary academic trend (limited to communication major) of business communication teaching in Korea to see how Korean academics perceive business communication. He tries to address the questions of which kinds of business communication Korean business communicators teach and which traditions they follow (i.e., American vs. European) in terms of administering web research (and phone calls with administers for the departmental registrar) and conducting related qualitative interviews with professors whose academic interests are related to business communication. He exemplifies that Korean business communication studies follow the American tradition (i.e., communication in business rather than communication for business) in that Korean business communication curricula are mostly composed of corporate communication (PR-related courses) and organization communication (with particular reference to media studies in the organization). In this respect, he claims that Korean academics take the local perspective of business communication in its definition, as courses in PR communication and media studies hold priority among others. This may cause a resulting instability of business communication curricula in Korean higher education. The outcome of Jung's (2018) web research clarifies the passive and/or unprestigious academic trend in Korean business communication. For instance, interview data illustrate that business discourse analysts who can deal with actual language data are extremely few in Korea. Also, the interviewed tenured Korean professors only considered part-time (or contract) instructors for business communication courses. No doubt, business communication classes are not compulsory, as Chang et al.'s (2018) results also show that business communication courses are electives. To a lesser extent, Jung (2018) tries to address how the teaching trend is projected to research trends in business communication in Korea in terms of online research on the Korean academic associations pertaining to the discipline of business communication. Major Korean communication associations with a relatively long history are still conservative regarding the discipline of business communication or do not consider the prestige of the field of business communication. For instance, business communication is nowhere in the Korean Society for Journalism and Communication Studies' 20 SIGs. The SIGs include some subdisciplines of business communication or professional communication though (e.g., organizational communication, international communication, PR, media studies, human communication, science, health, environment, and risk communication). Chang et al. (2018) and Jung (2018) believe that diachronic research on the fundamental reason for the sudden change in curriculum design will help locate the cause of the passive academic trend of business communication in Korean higher education. Chang et al. (2018) claim that a frequent restructuring of departments without consideration of a variety of factors (e.g., the factor of changing demands of industry) causes the limitations of curriculum instability in

Korean universities. Likewise, Jung (2018) illustrates that the fundamental reason for passive academic trends on business communication teaching in Korea needs to be explored by tracking curricular changes in a variety of institutional/departmental homes or locations of communication courses (e.g., communication/English departments and/or business schools) that are attributed specifically to their new standards or contemporary social demands. He claims that this investigation might be a stepping stone to fill the gap between the Korean academic tradition in business communication and their American and European counterparts. Chang et al. (2018) try to suggest a provision of a framework for a curriculum that addresses the needs of the stakeholders in the management process and improves communication in actual business contexts as the key conclusion is pinpointed. According to them, the curriculum is one of the main elements in education, and in order to achieve its goals, it needs to meet customer needs of business and education. To bridge the gap between academics and practitioners goes along well with KABC's mission. Namely, KABC aims to promote friendship between academic and industrial members. Furthermore, Jung (2018) claims that filling the gap with the fundamental reason for heterogeneity between the two parties is an urgent step before considering methods for designing new business communication curricula. It is because the Korean business professionals' way of interpreting workplace knowledge illustrates that there is a significant gap between academics and practitioners in Korea.

3.3   Suggestions for enriching Korean business communication teaching and research

Based on both Chang et al.'s (2018) and Jung's (2018) same key shared conclusions as user-oriented Korean business communication curriculum design, this chapter will end with some suggestions as guidelines for future research. In addition to overcoming heterogeneity between academics and practitioners, it is also necessary to break the wall between academic disciplines and actively study interdisciplinary higher education in Korea. For instance, diverse approaches to business communication research are needed in Korea. Business communication is more than the three prongs of advertising, public relations, and marketing communication, yet these three prongs continue to be prioritized due to the fact that the majority of communication-major (and business-major) faculty members in Korean universities are educated in American graduate schools where these prongs remain canon. I still remember hearing, 'There is no business communication in Korea', from a Korean interviewee for the CRARF project I conducted in Korea. Yet there are indeed business communicators in Korea. In fact, there are many, including media, advertiseming, and PR majors. It is more precise to say that there is no business-discourse-analysis track for business communication education. Efforts need to be made to embrace academic diversity to enrich Korean business communication education. As a suitable solution, more people who have studied authentic discourse analysis or languages for specific purposes at European universities adopting a broader scope of business communication (i.e., communication for business) should teach communication under the label of business communication. From the research aspect, likewise, newly established business-communication-related academic societies also need to make efforts to embrace a variety of business communication majors. Insofar as KABC is rooted in the American tradition of business communication centered on business administration, its name in Korean is *Kyengyengkhemwunikheysyenhakhoy* (Korean Association for Management Communication). This is clarified in its mission:

> contribution to the development of industry and the country by systematizing and disseminating the disciplines on *management communication*, which are essential for sustainable management of industries and companies, and contribution to the development of social public interest and *management communication* through research and international exchanges.
>
> (Emphasis in original.)

Another business-communication-related academic society, the Korean Association of English for Specific Purposes, or ESP Korea (http://esp-korea.org), recently established breakthroughs in practical English courses. It might be preferable to focus rather on local and professional languages for specific purposes to embrace academic diversity, with no limitation to English. It is urgent to settle the atmosphere to understand that English is one of the tools for communication. This is necessary for improving the quality of language education along with the aspect of embracing academic diversity. Also, it is critical for academia to pursue related fields of research. While there is hope and promise for the future, the field of Korean business communication faces obstacles and hurdles ahead.

References

Bargiela-Chiappini, F. (Ed.) (2009). *The Handbook of Business Discourse*. Edinburgh: Edinburgh University Press.

Chang, H., Park, P., & Cho, S. (2018). An analysis of business communication courses in business schools and suggestions for curriculum development. *Business Communication Research and Practice*, 1(1), 33–40.

Du-Babcock, B. (2018). Business communication research and theory development in Asia: Past, present, and future prospects. *Business Communication Research and Practice*, 1(1), 4–17.

Jung, Y. (2001a). *Giving bad news in Korean business communication.* Association for Business Communication Midwest, Eastern and Southeast conference. Kansas City, Missouri.

Jung, Y. (2001b). *Compliments in Korean business communication.* Association for Business Communication US West/Canada conference. Vancouver, Canada.

Jung, Y. (2001c). *Complaints in Korean business communication.* Association for Business Communication European convention. Technical University of Dresden, Germany.

Jung, Y. (2001d). *Politeness phenomena in Korean business communication: A global versus local view.* Association for Business Communication 66th annual convention. San Diego, California.

Jung, Y. (2002). *Requests in Korean business communication: A global versus local view.* Association for Business Communication European Convention. Aarhus School of Business, Denmark.

Jung, Y. (2004). *Polite disagreement in Korean business correspondence.* Association for Business Communication European convention, Catholic University, Milan Italy

Jung, Y. (2005a). *Politeness phenomena in Korean business genres* (Panel Presentation: Genre Use in Business Settings Across Countries). Association for Business Communication Asia and Pacific Convention. Chuo University, Tokyo Japan.

Jung, Y. (2005b). *Managing crisis communication in finnish and Korean undergraduates' case write-ups.* Association for Business Communication Annual Convention. Irvine, the US.

Jung, Y. (2005c). *The relativity of politeness in Korean business communication.* Association for Business Communication Annual Convention. Irvine, The US.

Jung, Y. (2009). Korea. In F. Bargiela-Chiappini (Ed.) *The Handbook of Business Discourse.* (pp. 356–371). Edinburgh: Edinburgh University Press.

Jung, Y. (2018). Trends in business communication research, teaching, and academic societies in Korean higher education. *Business Communication Research and Practice*, 1(1), 26–32.

Knight, M. (1999). Management communication in US MBA programs: The state of the art. *Business Communication Quarterly*, 62(4), 9–32.

Miller, K. (1996). Who are we and what are we doing? *Management Communication Quarterly*, 10(1), 3–4.

Watson, M. (2019). Identifying a key opportunity to grow the field in business communication. *Business Communication Research and Practice*, 2(2), 93–95.

4 Korean business politeness revisited

4.1 Lay concept of Korean politeness

Over the centuries, Confucianism came to constitute the basis of an Asian political ideal and to account for the mainstream of pre-modern philosophy in Korea. It thereby continues to exert a great influence on various facets of Korean history, culture, and social life. Confucianism is one of the chief factors that have determined traditional Korean patterns of thinking and action. It is certain that Confucianism continues to play an important role in Korea. Representative examples of the Confucianization process include Koreans' preference for sons, age-conscious relationships, a male-oriented society, and in-group-oriented interpersonal interaction, among others. Furthermore, Confucianism prescribes ideal human social relations across age, generation, gender, and status, establishing clear hierarchies between older and younger, and between male and female. This nature of Confucianism leads Koreans to be sensitive to the concepts of *cheymyen* ('face') and *yeyuy* ('decorum'). The primary generational ideology in Confucianism is filial piety. Filial piety assumes the enormous debt of children to their parents and, by extension, of people to their ancestors. It demands strict obedience, respect for authority, and careful care of parents and ancestors by offspring. Keeping this basic generational principle in mind, we turn to patrilineal kinship ideology. Korean patrilineal ideology maintains a strict hierarchy according to generation, birth order, and age. Those hierarchies are observed not only through kinship terminology but also through language use generally. The Korean language observes age hierarchy: verbs, forms of address, and vocabulary vary depending on who you are speaking to. Therefore, norms and values originating from Confucianism are able to account for how speakers make inferences about talking and for the construction of roles in interaction with others in Korea. In the light of Confucianism, the basic Korean cultural values/norms may be seen as collectivism, hierarchism, and indirectness. These social norms and cultural values reflect the aspect of politeness in Korea.

DOI: 10.4324/9781003108061-4

Therefore, being polite means generally conforming to socially agreed-upon codes (i.e., collectivism, hierarchism, and indirectness).

4.1.1   Collectivism

Korean is called a macro-to-micro language because 'the universe is represented in the order of a set (macro) and then its members (micro)' (Sohn 1999: 16). For example, Koreans put the family name first and then the given name second. Likewise, they write postal addresses following a sequence of bigger to smaller units. This macro-to-micro order reflects the collective nature of the Korean language. Numerous Korean terms carry a sense of interdependence and interrelatedness based on collectivism. For example, the concept of *hyoto* ('filial duty') refers to a particular relationship between parents and their children. Terms such as *hakyen* ('school ties'), *ciyen* ('regionalism'), and *hyelyen* ('ties of kinship') function as basic units of many social activities in Korea (e.g., business transactions and operations of companies' administrative culture). Due to the collectivistic nature of Korean society, Koreans commonly use kinship terms even between non-siblings. This is because the model of a strong family structure extends into social life. Koreans also prefer to use 'we' instead of 'I', as in 'our school' instead of 'my school', 'our house' instead of 'my house', and 'our department' instead of 'my department'. Using 'my' may give the impression that the speaker is arrogant. It may also be consistent with the lack of a sense of possessiveness stemming from collectivism in many Asian languages (Mulholland 1997). We can also observe Koreans' emphasis on mutual involvement and interest in others' business according to conversational routines, such as common greetings (e.g., *Etikaseyyo?* ['Where are you going'], *Etikassta oseyyo?* ['Where have you been?'], *Cinci capswusyesseyo?* ['Did you eat your meal?']). Koreans tend to read the in-group members' feelings to maintain affective relations with in-group members in many interpersonal settings by following an affective communicative style, as shown in *Hanpencwumyen ceng epsta* ('Affection cannot be had by giving only once') and *Cengttaymwuney* ('Because of affection'). Similarly, Koreans value *nwunchi* (reading another's face [lit. 'eye measure']) so as not to hurt another's feelings (see Chapter 5 for more detail). A variety of nonverbal patterns also reflect collectivism in Korea. Rather than following the custom of dutch treat, one person normally pays for others in Korea. In having a meal, Koreans share a pot stew called *ccikay*.

4.1.2   Hierarchism

Koreans are sensitive to hierarchy; as the saying goes, *Chanmwulto wi alayka issta* ('There is order even when drinking cold water'). Based on hierarchism in Korea, an inferior will never use the first name of a superior as a term of address in normal Korean settings. Instead, the inferior may use the title with the last name or the title only to the superior. Koreans try not to use any of the second-person pronouns to superiors, either. An inferior tends to avoid using 'we' to include a superior. Suggestive expressions are not normally used to describe one's superior in Korea. Typically, seniors rarely express certain acknowledgments, such as thanking or apologizing, to their inferiors. By the same token, Koreans view age as one of the primary criteria for showing deference and in the choice of honorifics, address terms, and speech levels – that is, six addressee honorifics: -*ta* (plain), -*e* (intimate), -*ney* (familiar), -*(s)o* (blunt), -*(e)yo* (polite), -*(su)pnita* (deferential). For example, using proper kin terms is strictly observed even between twins. Nonverbal behavior also reflects hierarchical communicative patterns in Korea. When having a meal, a lower-status person should wait until a higher-status person starts eating, and a lower-status person should not finish eating earlier than a higher-status person does. When drinking with a superior, a subordinate hides his glass and turns away from the superior, and smoking in front of a superior is not allowed. Koreans use both hands when giving to or receiving something from a superior. Bowing to a superior is a common greeting in Korea.

4.1.3 Indirectness

Koreans are rather indirect in communicative behavior. Any disagreement made baldly may imply hostility in a normal Korean context. Instead, it is considered a virtue not to explicitly express one's opinions or feelings but to show humility or modesty. It may be consistent with the claim that the 'expressive' acts in Korea (e.g., thanking, congratulating, giving condolences, etc.) are not as expressive as in English in the frequency of use. Therefore, for example, thanking is quite limited among Koreans. Koreans are likely to reject positive evaluation, such as a compliment. Overt condolences are also quite rare. At best, one may indirectly say *Tulil malssumi epssupnita* ('I have no words to express'). Furthermore, Koreans' 'yes' does not necessarily signal agreement but may imply the meaning of 'I see' or 'Let me think', depending on context. Koreans understand such responses as saving each other's faces and thereby maintaining harmony. Maintaining the other's face or self-esteem may require attention to the state of the hearer's inner feelings. Besides, modesty is highly valued in Korea. Certain expressions based on modesty social norms in Korea are superficially illogical but pragmatically well-formed. Such expressions imply that Koreans consider humbleness as a social virtue. For example, when inviting someone into one's own house, he or she may say *Nwuchwuhaciman tuleoseyyo* ('Although the house is dirty, please come in') before dinner, Koreans may also say *Masun epsciman manhi tuseyyo* ('The food does not taste good, but help yourself') or *Mekulken epsciman manhi tuseyyo* ('There is nothing to eat, but help yourself'), and when offering a gift, the gift-giver may say *Yaksohaciman patuseyyo* ('This is nothing good but please take it'). Furthermore, the most frequent compliment response with a simple 'no' in Korea also denotes the complimentee's modesty, not a matter of a face-threatening act. Status difference also affects indirectness in linguistic behavior in Korea. When an inferior asks a question to a superior about private matters (e.g., age), he or she does so in terms of indirect speech acts that are phrased idiomatically. For example, *Olhay ettehkey toyseyyo?* ('What is . . . this year?'; lit. 'How does it become this year?') is a formula for asking for the superior's age indirectly.

4.2   Indirectness as the primary value of politeness

Over the last few decades, indirectness has been one of the most popular and universal cognitive values across cultures in studies on cross-cultural communication (Gesteland 1999; Hofstede 2001). It also becomes a crucial (non)linguistic feature or convention for politeness across cultures. Since directness is characterized as intrinsically face-threatening or impolite in sensitive/negative messages, it is necessary to be indirect for politeness purposes. Major politeness scholars (Lakoff 1973; Leech 1983; Brown and Levinson 1987) have carried out research on the realization of politeness strategies in making face-threatening messages more implicit or less explicit. In this respect, directness and indirectness are likely to be interpreted as the degree of clarity in face-threatening acts (FTAs). One of the most well-known research studies on strategic politeness is Brown and Levinson's (1987) theory of politeness. The concepts of positive and negative faces are essential in their theory. A positive face is defined as a want to be desirable to others, while a negative face is defined as a want to not to be impeded by others. Brown and Levinson call certain kinds of acts FTAs that challenge 'face wants.' Some acts (e.g., request, order) impose on the hearer's negative face by showing that the speaker gets the hearer to do something. Other acts (e.g., disagreement, complaint) threaten the hearer's positive face by indicating that the speaker does not share the hearer's wants. They classify politeness strategies in ascending order based on their indirectness, from the least indirect to the most indirect (i.e., bald on record, positive politeness, negative politeness, off-record, don't do the FTA). In strategic politeness, indirectness has been defined as a set of politeness strategies used to avoid or minimize FTAs on the hearer. Many business communication studies have used insights from Brown and Levinson's politeness theory. Ehlich and Wagner's (1995) edited volume for a discourse of business negotiation includes several pieces of research work on business negotiations using Brown and Levinson's framework: Grindsted (1997) explored the use of jokes as a strategy for creating solidarity and affiliation in Spanish and Danish negotiations. Van der Wijst and Ulijn (1995) analyzed polite linguistic behavior in the different stages of simulated negotiations in French between Dutch and French negotiators. Villemoes (1995) compared facework in naturally occurring Spanish and Danish negotiation data. Also, Van der Wijst (1996) explicated the relationship between facework and contextual factors (e.g., power and distance) in Dutch business negotiations to test the predictions of politeness theory. Charles (1996) investigated face-saving hedging devices in authentic English business negotiations to arrive at an explanation for buyer and seller behaviors. More recently, Planken (2005) focused on aspects of rapport management in simulated intercultural business negotiations involving ELF in terms of Brown and Levinson's taxonomy of politeness strategies. Besides business negotiation settings, comprehensive literature on requests in politeness enactment has also been built up (Pilegaard 1997, among many others). Pilegaard (1997) explained how the distribution of positive and negative politeness varies in requests in British business letters. He maintained that the quantity of positive politeness strategy decreases when the realization of negative politeness strategy increases during the course of business. All these studies tend to stick to Western orientation in an effort for politeness exclusively in negative/conflict (rather than positive/welcome) situations. Namely, until recently, the majority of linguistic politeness research has been restricted to the Anglo-Saxon research tradition mainly focusing on strategic politeness. Specifically, indirectness has been an important norm or value for strategic politeness (e.g., employing formulaic or conventional expressions to be conventionally indirect, such as want or anticipation statement in request, or making a non-conventionally indirect rejection by offering an alternative or giving overwhelming reasons). In this occasion, indirectness is an equivalent term to ambiguity or vagueness in strategic politeness. That is, how much unclear the speaker's/writer's negative/sensitive talk is the major criterion for politeness. This chapter, based on Jung's articles on indirectness in Korean business communication (Jung 2009a, b, c; 2010), examines whether the value of indirectness in Western politeness is equally applicable to Korean business politeness. It explores whether indirectness is inherent to Korean speech, and addresses whether politeness strategies are necessarily interpreted within the framework conditions of ambiguity/hesitation and politeness. It explicates the Korean perception of politeness and its link to directness and/or indirectness from a local perspective. It also investigates the intercultural perception of Korean business politeness to a minor extent in order to illustrate the link between directness and impoliteness.

4.2.1   Indirectness is ambiguity?

Even in cases where the other party is rhetorically straightforward, Koreans try to avoid confrontation strategically. Due to the prevalent tendency of indirectness in Korea, instead of saying 'no', one may use such an expression *Himtulketkathay* ('It seems difficult'). In an empirical study of indirect speech acts, Jung (2009a) investigates requests in Korean business correspondence with particular reference to Brown and Levinson's theory of politeness. Communication strategies for requests, which appear in Korean business correspondence, are as follows: (1) conventional indirectness (want statements [e.g., *I hope you will check it with the support team*] and conditional appreciation [e.g., *I would appreciate it if you would consider our situation and continue to comply with the terms of the existing contract*]); (2) mitigating devices (hedges [e.g., *It seems that the shipping date should be delayed for a week only because of the circumstances on the spot*] and overwhelming reasons [e.g., *Since the decision was made after operating the production line, I request that you conduct an investigation again*]); (3) defocusing the writer/reader from the FTA (pluralization of the 'I' pronoun [e.g., *I inform you that, because of our firm's regulations, it is difficult to accept the settlement condition of 120 days that you requested*], using occupational terms [e.g., *I ask you to take quick action after checking if you, the designer, made a mistake in your work*], and nominalization [e.g., *I ask your reconsideration of a price increase*]); (4) off-record (reasonableness [e.g., *I need to bring them to the sales office before Thanksgiving Day*] and act in question [e.g., *Has this month's closing balance been calculated? Finish it definitely by today*]). Jung (2010) also exemplifies that Korean employees show indirectness with individuality in their messages, incorporating a variety of sentence opening structures in terms of small talk. Korean businesspeople tend to avoid conflict and a lot of extra talk before getting down to business. Jung (2009b) claims that most requests are placed toward the end of the text. This is due to the fact that the rhetorical structure of Korean text is inductively oriented. In a hierarchical society (e.g., Korea), relative power is given more weight in determining variation in linguistic behavior, including the use of politeness strategies. In this respect, communication strategies are very likely to be most frequently used across companies and genres when the reader is more powerful. All these Korean politeness phenomena support the claim that cultural values significantly affect verbal (and nonverbal) business communication in Korea. However, exceptions running counter to cultural values can also be expected (Jung 2009b).

For instance, Jung (2009a) illustrates that powerful people prefer the use of the off-record strategy across companies and genres (e.g., asking a question is a request). Possibly, this is due to the fact that less powerful people quickly understand unconventional indirect utterances made by more powerful people in a 'standard situation', such as a business office. According to Jung (2009a), furthermore, the off-record strategy is used most frequently when the distance between interactants is small. It shows that interactants are close enough to share common knowledge. In this occasion, indirectness *is* clarity. An implicit message is not likely to be implicit but rather explicit, as far as the implicit message is repeatedly given in a conventional situation. This finding shows that some politeness strategies for requests employed in Korean business communication reflect cross-cultural differences. That is why the conceptualization of 'face' has been challenged by some East Asian scholars (Matsumoto 1988; Ide 1989; Mao 1994) because Brown and Levinson (1987) are not much concerned about social identity, which is highly appreciated in East Asia. Matsumoto (1988) and Gu (1990) argue that 'face' in Eastern cultures is not a matter of autonomy or imposition but rather a matter of harmony and disharmony. This argument proposes that we need a more balanced or integrated framework between negative and positive 'face wants'.

Jung (2009a) found that requests are not always considered a threat to the addressee's negative face but sometimes a way of creating solidarity in Korean culture, as in the case of using the off-record strategy as a shared knowledge for a request. That is one of the fundamental reasons for the allowance of a direct request. In this respect, the idea of making solidarity (i.e., positive politeness) and avoiding conflict (i.e., negative politeness) by using the same strategy (i.e., off-record) may constitute a new concept other than positive and negative politeness, so-called ambivalent politeness (Jung 2003).

4.2.2 *Politeness* is *a consideration?*

Jung (2010) illustrates that using email and telephone simultaneously is a well-known form of business politeness in Korea. This Korean business politeness is directly linked to the normativity of common-sense (or discernment) politeness (Ide 1989). According to Jung (2010), sending an email, and an email only, can be interpreted as a rather irresponsible and even rude form of behavior (especially between people of different statuses), so he or she needs to call the other party to check on whether they received the message or let them know that he or she just sent them an email. After sending an email, Korean employees typically confirm receipt of the message by following up with a phone call. Unless there is immediate acknowledgment from the receiving party, senders of email will automatically assume that their messages did not properly reach the other party. This convention can enable each one's positive face to be saved so that solidarity can be created. Accordingly, this interaction can be considered a ritual in that it enhances social membership or solidarity; otherwise, the mutual confidence and initiative of participants may be reduced (Goffman 1967). Speeds of interaction reinforce solidarity and eventual trust in that the message sender expects an immediate acknowledgment from the recipient. Korean employees get used to this *automatic reciprocity* in communication, even in the use of less rich media (i.e., email) instead of face-to-face communication. In light of communication channel use, however, this Korean perception of common-sense politeness can be interpreted in a self-oriented way. It is because the lay concept of politeness may seem like a contradiction. Politeness seems a contradiction because saving one's face is as important as saving another's face in many cases. As Jung (2010) clarifies, for example, whenever Korean employees need, they call others to discuss business matters. And they double-check on each stage of a business job out of concern that a message was not correctly received. Accordingly, Korean employees expect immediate acknowledgment from the other party. Likewise, Jung (2009a) claims that code-mixing can help protect one's face in that it shows his or her professional work ability to the unfamiliar reader. Hedges in FTA situations can also be self-face-protective devices because performing the FTAs is as serious a threat to the FTA doer's face as the damage done to the face by FTAs from others. Furthermore, if the speaker does not reduce the force of his or her acts threatening to the hearer's face, the hearer will certainly pay the speaker back by doing more serious and harsh FTAs to the speaker later on. Although requestive hints are given to attenuate the force of FTA, they can also function as pre-requests to reduce or avoid the possibility of the speaker's request being rejected. Fundamentally, the perception of saving one's face originates in a Korean cognitive value, as Jung (2010) clarifies in the high/low frequency of his survey answers. First, Jung's (2010) survey answer is closely associated with how much Korean employees are sensitive to another's feeling ('When I communicate, I try to make the other person feel good'). However, another's perspective is not often considered in the light of the low frequency of an answer ('When I communicate, I try to see the matter from the other person's perspective as well'). This survey result implies that Korean business politeness is, to some extent, self-oriented. In this respect, the concept of Korean business politeness does seem irrelevant to social interaction. Instead, politeness is a social act to protect one's face in Korean business communication. Absolute or automatic approach to strategic politeness is also a self-oriented perspective. This conceptual contradiction in the study of politeness may constitute a new concept other than politeness, such as rapport management (Spencer-Oatey 2008).

4.2.3   *A face-threat* is *impoliteness?*

Perception of politeness can be interpreted differently by people from different cultures. Jung (2010) exemplifies that the simultaneous use of communication channels in Korean business encounters may threaten Finnish businesspeople, as shown in the following interview with a Finnish manager:

> Korean employees are direct. Whenever they need, they call us to discuss business matters. And they always double-check on each stage of a business job. Phone calls might be disturbing our job.
>
> (Jung 2010: 12)

This interview illustrates that Korean businesspeople are not always indirect. Due to the goal-oriented characteristic of a company, the speaker's wants or needs are able to override face concerns about the hearer in order to achieve the corporate goal. According to Jung (2010), Finns do not expect an acknowledgment from the other party after sending an email message. In the event that they need an urgent response, they will explain the reason, but otherwise, they do not ask for an immediate answer. The message sender respects the other's negative face wants not to be imposed on by unnecessary or redundant business work (i.e., to double-check whether the message properly finds the other party or not to give pressure for a quick answer unless it is an urgent matter). This may also be the reason, unlike the popularity of email, the telephone is not popular in the Finnish workplace. All these intercultural communication differences suggest to us that we need something more than the 20th century's theory of 'modern' politeness, the so-called strategic politeness, to explain the addressee's perceptions of (im)politeness. It also claims that no linguistic structure is inherently polite or impolite (Fraser and Nolan 1981) because politeness needs to be judged or evaluated depending on contexts or components. Korean self-oriented perspective is relevant to absolute or automatic approach to politeness. Korean businesspeople look polite, according to Brown and Levinson's theory of politeness. However, a different perception of politeness across cultures makes Brown and Levinson's framework challenged by approaches that highlight social norms and the evaluative character of judgments on politeness (Watts 2003; Locker and Watts 2005). This argument proposes that politeness should be seen as reciprocal or relational work. Social appropriateness is related to hearer-oriented in that the hearer's expectations about politeness need to be met for communication success (Spencer-Oatey 2005, 2008). Furthermore, since face entails claims on the evaluation of others, it needs to be analyzed as an interactional phenomenon (Spencer-Oatey 2008). In this respect, subsequent discourse is of importance in politeness studies (Jung 2009c). This claim may also go along well with relational work (Locker 2004; Locker and Watts 2005) in that it not only refers to linguistic politeness but is meant to cover the entire spectrum of interpersonal linguistic behavior. It is a hallmark of rapport management related to one of the key functions of all languages, the management of social relations (i.e., the relative harmony and smoothness of relations between people) (Spencer-Oatey 2008). It is important to note that rapport management not only focuses on the negotiation of harmonious relations. It emphasizes interrelationship in terms of a balance between oneself and another. It is essential that people find a balance between their own conditions and their interlocutor's face condition for successful rapport management. In this respect, Korean business politeness in Jung's research (2010) seems like a violation of rapport management across cultures. This violation may link to rapport neglect orientation (Spencer-Oatey 2005: 96). When people hold a rapport neglect orientation, they have little or no concern for the quality of the relationship between interlocutors. This may happen when their attention is focused on transactional (i.e., task-oriented) matters or more on their own face sensitivities, sociality rights and obligations, and/ or interactional goals. However, rapport neglect in Korean business communication does not seem to be impolite in an intercultural business encounter, as shown in the following interview with a Finnish manager:

> Korean employees are direct. Whenever they need, they call us to discuss business matters. . . . Phone calls might be disturbing our job. However, to make a clear each stage of a job can make business more successful at last, because it minimizes miscommunication between the two.
>
> (Jung 2010: 14)

Korean employees' directness in business activities may threaten Finnish business professionals' negative 'face wants' to not to be interrupted, so a possible conflict is likely to arise. However, Jung (2010) sees that Finnish employees manage this conflict situation fundamentally through *differentiation* (e.g., clear understanding of differences, acceptance of other's positions as 'legitimate', interpreting behavior in terms of its causes). Finnish employees accommodate differences (i.e., differentiation) of Korean employees. This is to achieve the benefits of differentiation and to make a transition to *integration* (Fisher and Ury 1981; Pruitt and Carnevale 1993). As remarked in the interview ('to make a clear each stage of a job can make business more successful at last, because it minimizes miscommunication between the two'), differentiation can be a crucial benefit to achieve 'interactional goals' in the workplace (i.e., to avoid miscommunication, leading to eventual business success with acknowledgment of common ground and moves to solidarity enhancement [improving the harmony of the relationship]). Finnish employees do not judge or evaluate Korean employees' possible interruption negatively or impolitely but do consider it as 'unmarked rudeness' (Terkourafi 2008). There are times when a face-threat can be appropriate in case impoliteness is not intentional (Terkourafi 2008). In a similar vein, 'mock impoliteness' (Culpeper 1996) or 'sanctioned aggressive facework' (Watts 2003) refers to 'impolite behaviours that are not truly impolite but reflect the shared knowledge and values of group, and which have the effect and intention of reinforcing solidarity among group members' (Schnurr et al. 2008: 212). In this relative aspect of politeness and impoliteness, politeness theory needs to incorporate impoliteness (Culpeper 1996).

References

Brown, P., & Levinson, S. (1987). *Politeness: Some Universals in Language Use.* Cambridge: Cambridge University Press.

Charles, M. (1996). Business negotiations: Interdependence between discourse and the business relationship. *English for Specific Purposes*, 15(1), 19–36.

Culpeper, J. 1996. Towards an anatomy of impoliteness. *Journal of Pragmatics* 25(3), 349–367.

Ehlich, K., & Wagner, J. (Eds.) (1995). *The Discourse of Business Negotiation.* Berlin: Mouton de Gruyter.

Fisher, R., & Ury, W. (1981) *Getting to Yes: Negotiating Agreement Without Giving in.* Boston: Houghton Mifflin.

Fraser, B., & Nolen, W. (1981). The association of deference with linguistic form. *International Journal of the Sociology of Language*, 1981, 93–109.

Gesteland, R. (1999). *Cross-cultural Business Behavior: Marketing, Negotiating, and Managing Across Culture.* Copenhagen: Copenhagen Business School Press.

Goffman, E. (1967). *Interaction Ritual: Essays on Face-to-Face Behavior.* New York: Pantheon Books.

Grindsted, A. 1997. Joking as a strategy in Spanish and Danish negotiations. In F. Bargiela-Chiappini & S. Harris (Eds.) *The Languages of Business: An International Perspective.* (pp. 159–82). Edinburgh: Edinburgh University Press.

Gu, Y. (1990). Politeness phenomena in modern Chinese. *Journal of Pragmatics*, 14(2), 237–257.

Hofstede, G. (2001). *Cultures and Organizations* (2nd ed.). London: HarperCollinsBusiness.

Ide, S. (1989). Formal forms and discernment: Two neglected aspects of universals of linguistic politeness. Multilingua. *Journal of Cross-Cultural and Interlanguage Communication*, 8, 223–248.

Jung, Y. (2003). *The use of (im)politeness strategies in Korean business correspondence*. The University of Edinburgh PhD Dissertation.

Jung, Y. (2009a). Indirect Requests in Korean Business Correspondence. In W. Cheng & K. Kong (Eds.) *Professional Communication: Collaboration between Academics and Practitioners*. Hong Kong: University of Hong Kong Press.

Jung, Y. (2009b). Korea. In F. Bargiela-Chiappini (Ed.) *The Handbook of Business Discourse*. Edinburgh: Edinburgh University Press.

Jung, Y. (2009c). A review of theory of rapport management. In L. Louhiala-Salminen & A. Kankaanranta (Eds.) *The Ascent of International Business Communication*. Helsinki School of Economics Press.

Jung, Y. (2010). Perceptions of (in)directness in Finnish and Korean business interaction *The Journal of International Business Communication*, 69.

Lakoff, R. (1973). *The logic of politeness: Or minding your p's and q's*. Proceedings of the Ninth Regional Meeting of the Chicago Linguistic Society, 292–305.

Leech, G. (1983). *Principles of Pragmatics*. London: Longman.

Locher, M. (2004). *Power and Politeness in Action: Disagreements in Oral Communication*. Berlin: Mouton de Gruyter.

Locher, M., & Watts, R. (2005). Politeness theory and relational work. *Journal of Politeness Research*, 1(1), 9–33.

Mao, L.R. (1994). Beyond politeness theory: 'Face' revisited and renewed. *Journal of Pragmatics*, 21, 451–486.

Matsumoto, Y. (1988). Reexamination of the universality of face: Politeness phenomena in Japanese. *Journal of Pragmatics*, 12, 403–426.

Mulholland, J. (1997). The Asian connection: Business requests and acknowledgements. In F. Bargiela-Chiappini & S. Harris. (Eds.) *The Language of Business: An International Perspective*. Edinburgh: Edinburgh University Press.

Pilegaard, M. (1997). Politeness in written business discourses: A textlinguistic perspective on requests. *Journal of Pragmatics*, 28(2), 223–244.

Planken, B. (2005). Managing rapport in lingua franca sales negotiations: A comparison of professional and aspiring negotiators. *English for Specific Purposes*, 24(4), 381–400.

Pruitt, D.G., & Carnevale, P.J. (1993). *Negotiation in Social Conflict*. Pacific Grove, CA: Brooks/Cole.

Schnurr, S., Meredith, M., & Holmes, J. (2008). Impoliteness as a means of contesting power relations in the workplace. In D. Bousfield & M. Locher (Eds.) *Impoliteness in Language: Studies on Its Interplay with Power in Theory and Practice* (pp. 211–229). Berlin: Mouton de Gruyter.

Sohn, H-M. (1999). *The Korean Language*. Cambridge: Cambridge University Press.

Spencer-Oatey, H. (2005). (Im)politeness, face and perceptions of rapport: Unpackaging their bases and interrelationships. *Journal of Politeness Research*, 1(1), 95–119.

Spencer-Oatey, H. (2008). Face, (im)politeness and rapport. In H. Spencer-Oatey (Ed.) *Culturally Speaking: Culture, Communication and Politeness Theory* (2nd ed., pp. 11–47). London: Continuum.

Terkourafi, M. (2008). Toward a unified theory of politeness, impoliteness, and rudeness. In D. Bousfield & M. Locher (Eds.) *Impoliteness in Language: Studies on its Interplay with Power in Theory and Practice* (pp. 45–74). Berlin: Mouton de Gruyter.

Van der Wijst, P., & Ulijn, J. (1995). Politeness in French/Dutch negotiations. In K. Ehlich & J. Wagner (Eds.) *The Discourse of Business Negotiations* (pp. 313–348). Berlin: Mouton de Gruyter.

Van der Wijst, P. (1996). *Politeness in requests and negotiations*. Ph.D. Dissertation. Katholieke Universiteit Brabant.

Villemoes, A. (1995). Culturally determined facework priorities in Danish and Spanish business negotiation. In K. Ehlich & J. Wagner (Eds.) *The Discourse of Business Negotiations* (pp. 291–312). Berlin: Mouton de Gruyter.

Watts, R. (2003). *Politeness*. Cambridge: Cambridge University Press.

5 Korean service encounters

The term *service encounter* refers to social interaction in commercial and non-commercial settings. The genre of service encounters comprises 'a class of communicative events, the members of which [service-provider and service-seeker] share some set of communicative purposes' (Swales 1990: 58). Traverso (2001) proposes a typology of service encounters: (i) open/closed settings (e.g., corner shops vs. open-air markets), (2) types of products purchased, (3) the type of sales outlet (e.g., self-service stores vs. other venues), (4) a designated physical setting versus an ambulatory setting (e.g., grocery store vs. selling candies to passengers on a bus), and (5) spatial characteristics (e.g., facility of circulation). Service encounters consist of interactions in both formal (e.g., emergency calls or telephone service calls, the so-called *e-service encounter*, used to refer to sales transactions between customers and service providers engaged in online interactions) and non-formal contexts (e.g., markets and small shops). In designated settings, participants engage in relational work to negotiate a sales transaction (exchange of goods) in order to achieve a common communicative purpose: 'demanding and giving goods & services' (Ventola 1987: 115).

This chapter covers facilities in fixed locations. The majority of the settings are covered facilities in fixed locations. This chapter examines commercial settings that require monetary exchange to finalize the transaction. It also emphasizes no payment sequence (non-commercial setting [request for information]). Non-commercial settings comprise information centers, library reference desks, student exchange offices, and hospital information desks. Some selective cultural elements achieving customer satisfaction are explored (i.e., cultural variation [e.g., variation according to the setting, the interaction, participants' roles, sequential organization of the sales transaction, and relational talk] and politeness norms). The top-down approach is characterized by the analysis of discourse patterns (phrases of the transaction), the generic structure (obligatory elements), and discourse strategies (e.g., repair, politeness). Ventola (1987) claims that non-transactional talk,

DOI: 10.4324/9781003108061-5

such as the relational talk of greetings and small talk and metalinguistic discourses, is important for the outcome of the interaction because it promotes and maintains interpersonal relations between the participants. Forms of address are devices that refer to the addressee and are studied under person and social deixis. Person deixis concerns the identification of the addressee or participant roles and is commonly realized through personal pronouns and vocatives (e.g., titles, kinship terms, and proper names). Social deixis is expressed through the codification of the social status between speaker and addressee(s) or speaker and some referent (Levinson 1983: 63). In this chapter, nevertheless, interactions in commercial and non-commercial settings do not include non-transactional talk that is embedded in the transaction. This chapter does not look at the overall organization of the encounter (generic structure; top-down approach) and the sequential structure of social actions (e.g., openings and closings, request-response sequence; bottom-up approach). It is mainly about the last phase of the service sales manual that consists of handling complaints from customers and malicious customers. It centers on the negative aspect of the interaction, that is, how service encounters are perceived as unsuccessful (e.g., passengers who sent complaint letters to an airline). It focuses on issues of customer dissatisfaction with the product received (Gutek 1995; Gutek et al. 1999).

The following section explores the role of empathy in managing the client's complaint.

5.1 Korean empathy

A useful distinction in discussions of workplace discourse is that of transactional and interpersonal (or relational) language and goals (Halliday 1978, 1985; McCarthy 1998; Coupland 2000; Holmes 2000; Koester 2004, 2006; Mirivel and Tracy 2005). People have goals during communicative interaction, and the goals can affect rapport management judgments. According to Spencer-Oatey (2008), interactional goals are goals in interaction that participants may have (i.e., transactional and relational). McCarthy's (2000) distinction between four types of talk in his analysis of service encounters seems useful:

1   Phatic exchanges (greetings, partings)
2   Relational talk (small talk, anecdotes, wider topics of mutual interest)
3   Transactional-plus-relational talk (non-obligatory task evaluations and other comments)
4   Transactional talk (requests, inquiries, instructions)

McCarthy's noteworthy claim in his classification is that although a distinction can be made between transactional (i.e., task-oriented) and relational goals (Brown and Yule 1983), types of communicative goals are interconnected. This is because transactional goals can be achieved based on the proper management of relational goals. McCarthy notes that, even in transactional talk, participants still 'reinforce the relational context' (ibid.: 104) through interpersonal choices (Halliday 1985), such as pronouns (for example, communal *we* rather than *I* or *you*), and Koester (2006, 2010) methodically explores such features in workplace contexts. Interpersonal, relational elements are visible at the lexico-grammatical level and at the turn and sequence level. Relational or social talk plays a significant role by enhancing rapport among colleagues and thus contributing to positive workplace relations (Holmes and Stubbe 2003). It helps to create team spirit by expressing solidarity or a sense of group belonging (Fletcher 1999). It manages power relationships among team members by deemphasizing power differences (Brown and Keegan 1999). Empathy talk supports an existence of a continuum between relational talk and transactional talk, which is McCarthy's (2000) transactional-plus-relational talk, due to its overlapping function between relational talk and transactional talk. Hogan (1975) captured the essence of call center interactions in his description of the empathic speaker and listener. An empathic 'actor' will typically *tailor* his or her performances to the needs and requirements of his or her audience; the actor will also tend to be an effective speaker as a result of an ability to anticipate the informational requirements of his or her listener (p. 15; emphasis is given). Simply learning and repeating formulaic expressions of empathy may undercut its contribution. The fact that empathic needs are different from customer to customer leads us to propose that just learning ways to express empathy is not sufficient for success; rather, agents are tactically taught to do empathy work. Empathy's full potential for contributing to customer service at call centers requires not only knowing expressions of empathy but also making decisions about their use based on customer needs. Empathy work involves discerning the appropriateness of empathy for each customer in order to determine whether and how to use it. Agents tailor responses to meet customers' needs expeditiously. In this respect, empathy should have multiple meanings that have been conceptualized variously (Clark 2007: xii). It is defined as listening attentively to assess the need for empathy and providing the necessary communicative responses to meet that need expeditiously (Clark et al. 2013). Agents enact empathic communication by listening closely to customers (attentive empathy), offering emotional support (affective empathy), and anticipating needs (cognitive empathy). This scientific notion of empathy looks far different from the lay concept of empathy in Korea, *kamcengiip* (感情移入) or *kongkam* (共感), which is defined under a narrow scope of mainly emotion-oriented empathy, so-called affective empathy. Affective empathy has been defined as identifying with what another person is feeling or responding with the same emotion as that of the other person (Aggarwal et al. 2005; Clark et al. 2013). Service agents express affective empathy by offering emotional support. Let us explore Korean empathy, under the label of affective empathy, with example 1, a customer's complaint about a travel agency's dissatisfied service.

Example 1

> It was a trip I was hoping for such a long time, but it was so different from the reservation details, ①so that it was ridiculous.
> What do you mean by ridiculous?
> The meal wasn't special, and I didn't get the massage properly.
> ②That's what you should have asked right there. It is a package that provides both foot and shoulder massage.
> I told the tour guide that I was booked for a full body massage, but they told me that it was just cut off to get a foot massage.
> If you appeal enough on the spot, the guide should contact us right away . . . ③Looks like you're not doing that!
> Hey, I'm not doing this for a few pennies right now. ④Put yourself in my shoes.
> Don't be angry. Listen to my explanation.
> Oh my, did I get angry? Hey, ⑤think about how you feel if you're a customer. ⑥It's as if you're telling me that I was wrong.
> I don't mean that.
> What is it not? In the end, you make me remember all the bad memories.

The customer is upset from the beginning of the phone call (①*so that it was ridiculous*). It is a long-awaited trip, and the customer is not in a good mood because of ruining it. Although the customer tends to invite (affective) empathy (i.e., *Put yourself in my shoes; think about how you feel if you're a customer*), the agent does not show empathy back to her, but instead, she simply rejects the customer's wish to seek agreement. The travel agent tends to shift the blame to the customer, as remarked in ②*That's what you should have asked right there* and ③*Looks like you're not doing that!* Besides a complaint about the service quality of the agency during her travel, this makes the customer initiate another kind of complaint in ⑥*It's as if you're telling me that I was wrong*, a complaint about the counterpart's way or attitude of complaint management. In the context of service encounters, it is certain that dispreferred responses do not seem to be perceived as impolite because the clerk's negative response is in accordance with the rules of the institutional setting (so-called unmarked rudeness) – that is, dispreferred response represents an appropriate response and is not viewed as a face-threatening act. However, a dispreferred response can represent a threat to the interlocutor's positive face (dissociation of the face) (Brown and Levinson 1987). Therefore, dispreferred responses are prefaced (or delayed) by various components (mitigated elements), such as positive remarks (e.g., 'it's a good idea, but . . .'), pro forma agreements (e.g., 'yes, but . . .'), hedges (e.g., 'probably', maybe'), epistemic expressions (e.g., 'I think', 'I believe'), silence, and often include elaborations or accounts (Pomerantz 1984). Besides those conventional language devices for buffering possible threats to the interlocutor's face, affective empathy may serve the same function in Korean service encounters. Affective empathy – stating understanding, offering apology, or referencing what others have experienced – is sometimes less than expected, and this kind of empathy is often not essential, even for customers in personal distress. The agent is generally not concerned about the customer's feelings or emotions but the situation from his or her point of view. He or she explains the situation objectively without sharing the customer's feelings. The transactional communication suggests that the agent should make and support reasonable arguments using claims and evidence to achieve business goals and, to a lesser extent, build personal credibility, appeal to organizational credibility, or appeal to the emotion of the audience (Jung 2017). Not all customers may seek or need empathy either. Some may want to avoid it completely, preferring an objective answer. But after agents express affective empathy, some customers may move to the core issue motivating their talks, which suggests that affective expressions may help move some talks toward resolution. In this respect, Giese and Cote (2000) conceptualized customer satisfaction to be an emotional or cognitive response, with a focus on subjective perspectives such as customer expectations and experiences. They also claimed that the response occurred not only when using the service but also after decision-making, after purchase, or even after several experiences. Therefore, it seems necessary to focus on the customer's response and experience at the time of service delivery during the development of the service sales, reinforce the customer's positive experience, and improve the behavior and dialogue technique of employees to minimize a negative experience. Empathy communication may be necessary or appropriate and play a selective but highly significant role in service encounters. This is because the emotional 'audience person' tend to be an untactful and inappreciative listener, becoming passive and discouraged in their performances in a response to non-empathic actor (i.e., empathyless agent) exclusively in the position of avoidance of his or her organization's wrongdoing, thereby not providing an accepting and generally not rewarding context for interaction (Jung 2020).

As in the previous example, the nervous customer invites empathy toward the end of the conversation in example 2, the case of the customer's request for an exchange of his recently purchased mobile phone with a new one.

Example 2

Free exchange is possible within 14 days. But two days have passed.
Oh my, two days have passed? There was also the New Year holiday, so you have to take it into account. It's been only two days, but you shouldn't ask me to get A/S.
Of course, ①we want to exchange it!
Then do it!
Of course, ②we'd like to do it, but it's difficult because ③we operate according to the regulation of our headquarters. Since we also open during the New Year holidays, if you gave us a call, we could extend the grace period. However, ④you didn't contact us, so there's no way.
Then you can give me a grace period now!
Of course, ⑤we want to do that. But now, the computation itself is not possible at all!
I don't know that. Please!
Of course, ⑥we would like to do that, but –
Stop saying that you want to do it. Why don't you contact the head office? If I just say it's within 14 days, is it all over? I should say that if the holiday period is so long, of course, the holiday period should not be included! ⑦Put yourself in my shoes.

The customer is nervous because a problem with his new mobile phone occurred shortly after he purchased the phone. It makes sense that it is unfair to say that free exchange is possible within two weeks because there is a holiday in the middle. From the customer's point of view, the compensation period has only been over two days due to the holiday season, but it will feel more unfair to have to request A/S. For such a customer, receiving A/S can be overkill. Although the nervous customer invites empathy toward the end of the conversation (⑦*put yourself in my shoes*), the agent does not resonate with the customer's feelings. Instead, the service provider in example 2 tends to avoid responsibility by giving an overwhelming reason for rejecting the customer's request for a free exchange with a new mobile phone (③*because we operate according to the regulation of our headquarters*). As in the previous example, the service provider has a tendency to shift the responsibility to the customer (④*you didn't contact us*).

Affective empathy can be more comforting to a customer than a vague apology. In Korea, people rarely express certain acknowledgments, like an apology, because an apology implies an acknowledgment of the apologizer's lesser power over the apologizee. Due to their strong tendency to avoid overt apologies, people tend to make apologies indirectly in numerous ways. Sometimes the situation is exacerbated by habitual apology, such as *we want to do it* in ①, ②, ⑤, and ⑥. As for the content itself, it contains regret, so it may not be a big problem. Nevertheless, it can give the impression of avoiding problems. Although the service provider may really sympathize with his customer, he shouldn't repeat it just because he can't help it. It is a good idea to avoid showing excessive empathy and immersing in a customer's situation. This is because insincere empathy rather leads to counter-productivity.

In order to complement the pitfall of affective empathy, the role of cognitive empathy seems essential at service encounters. Cognitive empathy involves intellectually assuming the other person's perspective while retaining sufficient judgment to helpfully intervene. Agents express cognitive empathy by providing language that the customer needed, proposing options for eventualities that the customer might face, or stating what other customers have done. Agents use expressions of cognitive empathy to anticipate a customer's future needs and offer solutions in advance. Cognitive empathic responses have a greater effect on customer satisfaction than affective empathic responses. After each of these affective expressions, the agent immediately enacts cognitive empathy to meet the customer's informational needs. In this respect, Clark (2007) characterizes cognitive empathy as 'a mode of observation'. Cognitive empathic responses for finding the customer's future solutions do take time. Unlike affective empathy, which can be expressed immediately, cognitive empathy is said to require 'prolonged immersion in the broader perspective of a client's life' (Clark 2007). The path from resolution to complaint in a service encounter takes time from the macro issue of speech (i.e., mostly ending position in standard steps of service encounters). Agents consciously or subconsciously save resolution toward the end of the conversation. It supports the claim that cognitive empathic responses for finding the customer's future solutions do take time. When presenting a solution, the words that the customer is obligated to refer to it in advance make the situation remain intact in the past so that there is nothing to be solved. Sometimes the accused tend to simply deny any association with whatever is viewed negatively by the forceful customer. What happened is a thing of the past anyway, so customer service needs to keep it short, focusing on what can be done in the future. The way of trying to solve the problem and suggesting alternatives in the future may be more effective than repeating the words *I'd like to exchange it* or *I'm sorry.*

5.2 Nwunchi

As clarified in the previous section with the title of empathy, an overlapping function of relational talk with transactional talk is particularly important in Korea. It is due to the fact that the term 'hospitality culture' in reference to Korea means the practice of mixing business with the pleasure of entertainment. Entertaining and being entertained are essential parts of building a close relationship with Korean businesspeople. Before negotiating and entering into a business deal, Korean businesspeople socialize with potential partners and clients in order to establish a trusting relationship. This socializing is considered part of the 'work relationship', although no actual 'work' as it is understood in the West may be completed (i.e., clear-cut distinction between transactional talk and relational talk). The practice of mixing business with entertainment is also prominent inside the company. Events important to individual employees are acknowledged, and drinks are shared with co-workers (e.g., when he or she buys a new car or house), and your membership in a workplace automatically makes you important to your co-workers. This acknowledgment can be a signal of having *nwunchi*. Koreans value *nwunchi* (reading another's face or feeling [lit. 'eye measure']) so as not to hurt another's feelings or face but to save it. Being skilled at *nwunchi* is one of the important Korean business assets one can have, and such people are highly valued because they are the ones who help keep a workplace peaceful and collectivistic. In cultures with strong collectivist tendencies, it is common and familiar to live with care and attention.

Therefore, awareness is so important that sociality is determined by how fast it is noticed. Someone without *nwunchi* is a person who does not understand the atmosphere or situation in society and speaks wrongly. Basically, he or she does anything that does not fit into the mood and situation. He or she cannot read the other's nonverbal expressions (expression, posture, gaze, behavior, etc.) and the other's indirect language expressions. People without *nwunchi* are those who lack attention or do not understand the situation. In everyday life, words and actions without notice are close to words and actions that make the other person feel bad without being considerate of the other's feelings. People who do not notice are not ignoring the other person's position, but because they do not have the ability to judge at the moment that the other person will feel bad when they act in a certain situation. Usually, when it comes to being unnoticed, it has to do with how much we say or do that makes the other person feel bad. *Nwunchi* plays a key role in a high-context culture, a culture where communication highly depends on the situation and the speakers' relationships, as well as other things, including nonverbal communication. It is important to understand the meaning of what is said rather than just the words that are used. Example 3 is the case that the salesperson has no *nwunchi*. It is a sales talk in a used car market.

Example 3

On the internet, the price of the car was 30 million won, right? It's so cheap.

Oh, wait a minute! Check this out. That's 30 million won in cash. There is an additional 20 million won in the loan for this car.

Yeah? No, then ①tell me before I come out here. After I came out, now you told me that the car has a loan of 20 million won. Isn't it too much?

Oh, that's not what I sell directly.

What else does that mean?

There are some used cars that I sell and some that I only serve as bridges in the middle. I'm sorry anyway. There are a lot of good cars in the 30-million-won range, so I'll show you something else. Once you come out, you can compare them yourself, and ②it is important to come to visit a used car market.

Phew . . . Then, do you have imported cars in that price range as a hybrid?

③Oh, once you're out, aren't you going to see more vehicles?

④No, I wish it was a hybrid.

The cause of the problem in the example is that even though the customer's needs are clear, the obvious intention of the employee who wants to sell at least one car is persistent. And the intention is revealed as an attitude of continuing to push in without even knowing it. The customer is looking for a hybrid car with low fuel economy, but the salesperson says there are many other cars out there, so there is nothing to lose if the customer looks around, as remarked in ②*it is important to come to visit a used car market* and ③*Oh, once you're out, aren't you going to see more vehicles?* This is in total opposition to the customer's wish not to visit the market, as initiated toward the very beginning of the sales conversation (①*tell me before I come out here*). Salespeople inhibit surface listening and impatience, as empathy work requires paying close attention to determine customers' need for empathy. They demonstrate attentiveness in sales talk through behaviors associated with active listening, such as acknowledging, repeating, paraphrasing, elaborating the customers' ideas, summarizing, and asking questions. Salespeople are used to figuring out what they are asking for just by listening to the customer, so they might come up with a solution even before the customers are finished talking. It is time to look back to see if the customer was able to say what they wanted because of the salesperson's overeagerness to make a sale.

Salespeople use attentive responses to comprehend customers' needs, thereby providing timely service. Clark (2007) observes that 'empathy involves a commitment to grasp the internal state of an individual as accurately as possible'. This 'commitment to grasp' the customer's need for empathy requires actively listening for clues. The salesperson signals that he is listening attentively by acknowledging what he hears, asking a clarifying question, and repeating information for the customer throughout the call. The cumulative effect of these attentive responses is to let the customer know that he has the salesperson's full attention. How well the salesperson understands and prepares his customers will determine the quality of his sales conversation. During the conversation in example 3, the customer, emphasizing low fuel economy and imported cars, is hesitant to the recommendations of the salesperson (④*No, I wish it was a hybrid*). If the customer is reemphasizing the low fuel economy and imports, it is necessary to find out whether the condition is an important factor that cannot be replaced by another one, and, if so, then why. To do that, it may be necessary to first grasp the intention with appropriate questions (e.g., 'Is it important to have low fuel economy?'). The salesperson can find out whether the customer has a lot of work to drive for a long period of time or if it is for frequent travel purposes. The salesperson can also explore why the car must be imported, suggesting possible alternatives less important than these two factors, and broaden the customer's options. For example, if it is not necessarily an imported car, the salesperson can recommend that there are other vehicles with similar fuel economy conditions.

One of the easiest ways to build persuasive powers with prospects is being honest and doing what salespeople say they will do. Honesty is the best policy, and it is an effective way to build trust. The salesperson does not claim more than the product can accomplish. Salespeople provide an ethical service by telling the truth about what the product will do. A moral and ethical salesperson is certainly someone who will be faithful in taking care of customers. Because customers have many suppliers wanting to sell to them, they are impatient with salespeople who are unable to quickly demonstrate that they are knowledgeable business professionals. A competent salesperson knows a significant amount of product information. Today's salespeople are experts on a wide range of topics in order to be considered business consultants by their customers. People are going to buy what the salespeople offer only if those things make a positive difference to them. They are going to use the salesperson's services only if he or she somehow will improve their life or circumstances. And people are going to be far more inclined to share high-quality information with him or her if he or she shares some quality information with them. This requires information. What the seller obtains is professional knowledge about sales product (knowledge about product [e.g., performance data; physical size and characteristics; how the product operates; specific features, advantages, and benefits of the product; how well the product is selling in the marketplace]). The requirement of professional knowledge is relevant to knowledge-based trust (Candlin and Crichton 2013), trust based on the performance, knowledge, and proficiency or ability of others' actions (e.g., experience, accomplishment, education, membership, and reputation). Salespeople are not subjective but objective or relatively neutral for establishing credibility. They can provide a scientific result of the experiment to be objective in their sales presentation. Data should be the result of sufficient sample size and correct gathering and processing of them. Salespeople can use sales data such as test market information and current sales data. Industrial salespeople use performance data and facts based on company research as proof of their product's performance. Furthermore, proof furnished by reputable sources outside the company usually has more credibility than company-generated data. It must come from sources with experience or expertise in the area being discussed. For instance, pharmaceutical salespeople frequently tell physicians about medical research findings on their products published in leading medical journals by medical research authorities. Example 3 seems to be the case of lack of effort for establishing credentials in this respect. The salesperson said he was a middle seller and showed no responsibility, lowering his trustworthiness. The following two examples are also cases of lack of *nwunchi* in that the service agents fail to give proper answers to the customers due to careless listening.

Example 4

This product is a little weird.
 If you are going to receive A/S, write down the problems here.
 Even if that's not all about A/S, I'm going to ask a little.
 Then I will tell you the manufacturer's contact information.
 It's not that I haven't called.
 Then, I'll talk to the technician.
 Hey, <u>let me talk until the end. Why aren't you listening, huh?</u>

Example 5

> Is this card discounted at the hair shop?
> ①The card you mentioned is a discount card for gas stations and department stores.
> No, so is there a discount at the OO Hair Shop?
> As I mentioned, ②the card you have is a card that is mainly discounted at gas stations and department stores.
> So, in the end, ③there are no discounts, right? That's a lot of talk.
> Excuse me?

Responses from the agent seem solely based on his assumption in example 4, as not all the responses meet the customer's expectations. Namely, improper responses (i.e., suggestion to receive A/S even without asking about the problem once, provision of manufacturer's contact information to the customer, and delivery of the customer's message to the technician) are made without attentive listening to the customer's talk, as the customer's complaint is made at last (*let me talk until the end. Why aren't you listening, huh?*). Likewise, the call center agent in example 5 does not meet the customer's expectations. Certainly, call center operators are generally instructed to avoid using negative terms as much as possible. Therefore, it is hard to hear the word *no* in call center scripts. The goal of the call center is to lead the conversation with expressions such as *I will guide you where possible* rather than saying *no*. However, there are many cases where words that modify negative words are prolonged and lengthy, so counseling often becomes unpleasant. Therefore, the call center agent may decide to reduce the possibility of misunderstanding by saying *no* clearly. This depends on the case. For example, the customer in this example seems to be expecting a *yes* or *no* answer, as clarified in ③*there are no discounts, right?* Nevertheless, the agent twice gives a reason for a negative answer (①*The card you mentioned is a discount card for gas stations and department stores*; ②*the card you have is a card that is mainly discounted at gas stations and department stores*). From the perspective of politeness, it is an indirect disagreement using the off-record strategy, nonconventionally indirect disagreement, in that a negative answer is omitted right after the reason for disagreement (*therefore, the card is not discounted at the hair shop* or *there is no discount at the OO Hair Shop*). It illustrates that politeness is likely to be face-threat up to the audience's interpretation.

This finding supports the claim that good practice of business communication is highly context-sensitive. Communication is understood as social interaction (Nystrand 1987; Hyland 2000). Good business communication does not begin with an act of assertion (what the speaker thinks about his or her subject) but an act of listening (what others think). Speaking well means engaging the voices of others. This approach leads us to see speaking (even writing, depending on the situation) as an engagement in a social process. Namely, meanings and styles of communication can be socially mediated and influenced by the contextual or situational knowledge that speakers and hearers share in their discourse communities. In this respect, an objective of business communication is achieved by mutual agreement upon contextual or situational knowledge between interactants. This claim might go side by side with Hyland's (2000) notion of 'acceptability condition', statements incorporating an awareness of interpersonal factors principally in persuasion. In persuasive communication, a speaker not only wants his or her words to be understood (an illocutionary effect in speech-act terms) but also to *be accepted* (a perlocutionary effect or hearer action). This claim raises the issue of the relative or relational nature of communicative phenomena (surely including politeness phenomena). Similarly, discourse-functional grammarians (e.g., Chafe 1994, among many others) employ a conceptual tool such as 'information flow' to describe the dynamic nature of communication. Since the speaker takes the hearer's needs into account when producing discourse, the mental state of the hearer must be taken into account. Accordingly, hearer orientation needs to be emphasized in business communication research in that the hearer's expectation should be met for communicative success. It examines the claim that communicative behavior needs to be relational work. In other words, it also investigates the organizational members' perceptions or judgments of communicative behaviors (Spencer-Oatey 2008) in terms of the addressee's definition of (in)directness (Jung 2010).

Example 6, a call center conversation where the customer tries to check if points can be earned, is also the case of no *nwunchi*. It is a call center script. It superficially looks like a simple inquiry about the point earning. Like previous two cases, however, the customer's anger escalates in the end (③*Are you working properly?*).

Example 6

I bought it with a card at the OO Mart today, and the points were earned, right?

①There is no such event.

I beg your pardon? Apparently, it is known that 10,000 won points are provided when purchasing with an OO card at OO Mart.

---

②There is nothing announced on our side. Once again, please check with the mart.

I beg your pardon? ③Are you working properly? Why do I have to check this with the mart? ④The points that were applied to the car purchase last time weren't earned, either?

Sometimes lack of *nwunchi* is caused by professional knowledge. When service workers are stubborn and lazy and know less about discounts or accrual services than customers do, situations arise that upset customers. Of course, these days, there are so many different types of discount and saving services that it is difficult to know them all in advance. A key element of service is directly connected to reliability. If the agent repeats mistakes and inaccurate guidance, even his likability will plummet. Customers believe that the agent has almost all the information, so they expect him to guide them right away to the questions they ask. In example 6, the customer who participated in the event is deceived by a card company's call center agent, who appears to not know that he should have accumulated points by purchasing a card at at certain market. As a result, the customer now doubts that he received points as promised from purchasing a car. The word for the customer's feeling is *distrust*. Therefore, the response of blindly waiting or saying that the agent is not sure or the hasty response of pretending to know what he does not know well can be subject to complaints. By contrast, *trust* can help build and sustain favorable feelings between salespeople and customers. Therefore, call center agents ideally should update new information and announcements every day. However, these days, information-sharing and dissemination is so fast and indiscriminate, so more and more customers get information faster than call center agents. In service, accuracy and quick response are naturally required. However, accurate guidance is more important than quick guidance. This is because if the information that needs to be conveyed quickly is not accurate, it is useless. Therefore, the agents aim for promptness to answer immediately but do not hesitate to check and guide carefully if the content is confusing. In other words, the service provider seeks his patience before shouting for a moment without even attempting and tries to answer questions specifically and accurately at a time, even if it takes a while. If he is not in a situation where he can immediately check and respond, it is best to check and guide. There is a possibility that the event about accumulating the point is organized only in a particular supermarket so that the call center operator does not clearly make sense of it, as in ①*There is no such event* and ②*There is nothing announced on our side.*

This may make the customer's emotional response start with ③*Are you working properly?* That is why even her nonsensical inquiry, ④*The points that were applied to the car purchase last time weren't earned, either?*, is made to the present operator, in that the operator may be a different person from the one the customer talked to last time to ask the question. It sounds like a talk to invite (affective) empathy.

5.3   *Kapcil*

Standardization of services can prevent mistakes and deviations in providing customized services, maintaining reliability, helping management control, enhancing consumer protection, and raising confidence and satisfaction among consumers (Jones et al. 1994; Kasiri et al. 2017). Service companies develop the standard manual of customer service to train their employees to provide consistent service. In order to operate and manage the service process effectively and clearly, standards for service behavior and communication must be set for the employees to follow when responding to customers. However, *kapcil* customers may make talk in service encounters illogical, so the standardization of services is unlikely to be expected. For some time, Koreans have used the phrase, 'the person with a loud voice wins'. In many cases, it means that the opinions of the attacking person, who makes their assertions loudly and with yelling, are socially approved. The case is often seen where a loud screaming person wins in a controversy and in a debate, and even in a normal conversation in a quiet place, a loud-voiced person might dominant a meeting in Korea. We can often come across the voice of self-assertion by the drivers of two cars in a car accident on the road, an argument between a merchant who sells goods and a customer who buys goods, an argument between couples at home or on a bus or a train, or a public assembly where they push, pull, and step on their feet. In the quarrels in all these cases, the sound of the ritual rises and shouts come and go. In addition, even in a social gathering where friends, alumni, or co-workers gather, there are frequent situations in which they raise their voices by doing something that is not very trivial. Moreover, even at conference halls, seminar venues, parliaments and local councils, and even wedding halls and shopping centers, we can see a real scene of shouting and pointing. These unfavorable phenomena have become widespread, and the habit has been banalized. It is now perceived as a typical form of Korean behavior. The core of the problem is the perception of each citizen that it is advantageous to shout out their arguments aloud and the social climate in which such phenomena are positively accepted. This stereotypical form of Korean behavior is the origin of *kapcil* (lit. 'boss around'). *Kapcil* is an act to show a powerplay in *kapul* relations. The origin of *kapul* relations is that when writing a contract, *kap* is the one who takes the initiative in the contract relationship, and *ul* is the opposite person/party. In simple terms, *kap* is the one who is provided with goods or labor power by paying a remuneration, and the one who provides goods or labor by receiving a remuneration falls into *ul*. For example, in business-to-business transactions, the relationship between the customer and the sales company, the relationship between the main office and the subcontractor (supplier), the relationship between the employer and the employee in the business, and the relationship between the lender and the tenant in a lease contract. The culture of the *kapul* relations in Korea is usually thoroughly separated from the top and the bottom. Anyone who thinks they are a little higher than others expects that the subordinates should show a form of mental and physical obedience to authority. From this relationship, the term *kapcil* is also coined, meaning that a person located in a higher relationship in the contract (*kap*) makes an unreasonable or nonsensical request to a person located in a lower level (*ul*). There are many cases where *ul* were tolerated, and as this was repeated, more and more people tend to take *kapcil* as the 'natural' order of things. In the 21st century, when the word *kapcil* first started to spread, it originally referred to up-and-down relations by the power within the same organization or between different relationships. Formal institutional interactions are 'characteristically asymmetrical', and social interaction or dialogue at large 'must inevitably be asymmetric on a moment-to-moment basis' (Drew and Heritage 1992: 47–49). Service encounters are initially asymmetric due to the fixed structure of participants' roles (e.g., clerk and customer). Service encounters are asymmetric with regard to the participants' power of knowledge: the server knows information about the product and restricts the interaction to the sales transaction: the customer has the right to ask for a specific product, and the server has the responsibility to provide that service. In service industry, it is generally realized that the customer is king. The attitude that the customer is the king is a virtue that the seller should have, not the sentence that the buyer uses when he is truthful. Nevertheless, some Korean customers tend to take advantage of this good, faithful business maxim, so excessive truthfulness gradually becomes a social problem. Example 7 exemplifies *kapcil*. It is the case that the customer makes a complaint about a follow-up problem caused after the installation of the internet.

Example 7

Did you install the internet this morning?
    Anything wrong with your internet?
    No, the internet is fine, but there are other problems. I can't use fax.
    ①Obviously, it worked fine before you came.

Fax? I installed the internet.
②I can't use the fax after you installed the internet.
If it suddenly doesn't work, could it be that the line is loose?
It doesn't seem like a line problem. Then nothing else should be done. ③Obviously, you seem to have done something wrong while installing.
Oh, sorry. I'm not sure why. Anyway, I haven't touched anything else while installing the internet. What shall I do?
Then why is this? ④Since I can't use it after you have gone, please come back and see it.
Yeah? Should I? Phew . . . Okay, ⑤I'll call you later and visit you.

Even though there is no clear reason yet why the fax has a problem, the customer strongly believes that the problem is caused by the internet installer, as specified in ①*Obviously, it worked fine before you came*, ②*I can't use the fax after you installed the internet*, ③*Obviously, you seem to have done something wrong while installing*, and ④*Since I can't use it after you have gone*. It is certain that there is no scientific evidence to back up her assertion. Nevertheless, her assumption of doubting the installer seems to play a role in justifying her 'bald on-record' request at the end of the conversation (*please come back and see it*). She does not show any hesitation in her request. The 'bald-on-record' strategy involves performing face-threatening acts in the most direct way without redress. Since a request is inherently a face-threatening act, it is necessary to tone the request down for politeness purposes (Brown and Levinson 1987). The exceptional circumstances for the bald-on-record strategy for requests include only cases when the speech act is used mainly for communication efficiency (e.g., warning messages or instructions for taking medications). In example 7, although the customer has a right to ask for after-service on the internet only, she does even ask the installer to fix the fax. Since he has no obligation to fix it, her request is very likely to be an inconvenience to him. Her compelling request looks like *kapcil*. The service provider is responding to the needs of customers, but he should also include a confident attitude as a professional. Service agents can follow the procedure and process accordingly in the cases of a simple complaint, a complaint about the product and service, physical abuse, or a verbally abusive customer so that they can wisely solve problems rather than unconditionally apologize for every situation. The customer's *kapcil* may make him forget about this professionalism, but instead let him become subordinate to the customer's one-way wish, as remarked in ⑤*I'll call you later and visit you* in response to *please come back and see it*.

Example 8 also shows the use of a *kapcil*-type bald-on-record request. It is a scene of hassle in a cosmetic store. It is the case that the salesperson makes a rejection to the customer's request for an exchange of a purchased cosmetic item for fuller lashes with a new one for longer lashes, as the function of the purchased item is different from her expectation.

Example 8

What?

   Customer. Listen carefully to my explanation. ①This doesn't make the lashes longer, but it makes them look fuller.

   ②What's the difference between being rich [lush] and looking longer?

   What is rich is that it looks thick, but ③it does not mean that the lashes are longer.

   ④Oh, I don't know. ⑤I thought it made lashes longer, so I bought it, ⑥so change it.

The staff gives a reason for the rejection of the customer's request in ①, a functional difference (longer vs. fuller). Nevertheless, the customer tries not to accept the reason but instead asks a rhetorical question to make a disagreement with the staff in ②, no functional difference. Rhetorical questions do not necessarily solicit information or opinion. Their typical aim is to let the hearer know information, which is conveyed indirectly without telling the truth directly or trying to obtain an answer. The speaker tries to mirror the lack of clarity for politeness reasons. By doing face-threatening acts formulated as questions, the speaker tries to enable the hearer to interpret the intent of her face-threatening acts indirectly. Questions are devices to reduce the illocutionary force of face-threatening acts because although components (e.g., *differences* in example 8) are directly referred to, the illocutionary intent is not overtly stated in the sentence (i.e., *What's the difference between being rich and looking longer?* instead of *There is no difference between being rich and looking longer.*). The customer's rhetorical question seems like a 'mild hint' (Blum-Kulka and House 1989) in that the hint is formulated conventionally. The same reason for rejection to request is repeated in ③*it does not mean that the lashes are longer*. Lacking conscious awareness of attentiveness to the salesperson's explanation in ④*Oh, I don't know* supports to some extent the claim that the customer's question is not an authentic question for soliciting information but a rhetorical question for an indirect disagreement. Although the customer purchased the item owing to her misunderstanding, ⑤*I though it made lashes longer*, she stubbornly persists in an exchange using a bald-on-record strategy in ⑥*so change it*. Under the asymmetric relationship between customer and salesperson, the attitude of a customer who does not try to listen to words that are unfavorable to her and only asserts her own needs is certainly related to *kapcil*.

References

Aggarwal, P., Castleberry, S., Ridnour, R., & Shepherd, C.D. (2005). Salesperson empathy and listening: Impact on relationship outcomes. *Journal of Marketing Theory and Practice*, 13, 16–31.

Blum-Kulka, S., & House, J. (1989). Cross-cultural and situational variation in requesting behaviour. In S. Blum-Kulka, J. House, & G. Kasper (Eds.) *Cross-cultural Pragmatics: Requests and Apologies* (pp. 123–154). Norwood, NJ: Ablex.

Brown, G., & Yule, G. (1983). *Discourse Analysis*. Cambridge: Cambridge University Press.

Brown, R.B., & Keegan, D. (1999). Humor in the hotel kitchen. *Humor*, 12(1), 47–70.

Brown, P. and Levinson, S. (1987). *Politeness: some universals in language use*. Cambridge: Cambridge University Press.

Candlin, C.N., & Crichton, J. (Eds.) (2013). *Discourse of trust*. Basingstoke, Hampshire: Palgrave Macmillan.

Chafe, W. (1994). *Discourse, Consciousness, and Time*. Chicago: University of Chicago Press.

Clark, A.J. (2007). *Empathy in Counselling and Psychotherapy: Perspectives and Practices*. London. Lawrence Erlbaum Associates Publishers.

Clark, C.M., Murfett, U.M., Rogers, P.S., & Ang, S. (2013). Is empathy effective for customer service? Evidence from call center interactions. *Journal of Business and Technical Communication*, 27(2), 123–153.

Coupland, J. (Ed.) 2000. *Small Talk*. London: Longman.

Drew, P., & Heritage, J. (1992). Analyzing talk at work an introduction. In P. Drew & J. Heritage (Eds.) *Talk at Work. Interaction in Institutional Settings* (pp. 3–65). Cambridge: Cambridge University Press.

Fletcher, J.K. (1999). *Disappearing Acts: Gender, Power, and Relational Practice at Work*. Cambridge, MA: MIT Press.

Giese, J.L., & Cote, J.A. (2000). Defining consumer satisfaction. *Academy of Marketing Science Review*, 1(1), 1–27.

Gutek, B.A. (1995). *The Dynamics of Service: Reflections on the Changing Nature of Customer/Provider Interaction*. San Francisco, CA: Jossey-Bass.

Gutek, B.A., Bhappu, A.D., Liao-Troth, M.A., & Cerry, B. (1999). Distinguishing between service relationships and encounters. *Journal of Applied Psychology*, 84(2), 218–233.

Halliday, M. (1978). *Language as Social Semiotic: The Social Interpretation of Language and Meaning*. Baltimore, MD: Edward Arnold.

Halliday, M. (1985). *Spoken and Written Language*. Victoria: Deakin University.

Hogan, R. (1975). Empathy: A conceptual and psychometric analysis. *The Counselling Psychologist*, 5(2), 14–18.

Holmes, J. (2000). Doing collegiality and keeping control at work: Small talk in government department. In J. Coupland (Ed.) *Small Talk* (pp. 32–61). Harlow: Pearson Education.

Holmes, J., & Stubbe, M. (2003). *Power and Politeness in the Workplace*. London: Longman.

Hyland, K. (2000). *Disciplinary Discourse: Social Interaction in Academic Writing*. Essex: Longman.

Jones, C., Nickson, D., & Taylor, G. (1994). 'Ways' of the world: Managing culture in international hotel chains. In A.V. Seaton, C.L. Jenkins, R.C. Wood, P.U.C. Dieke, M.M. Bennett, L.R. MacEllan, & R. Smith (Eds.) *Tourism: The State of the Art* (pp. 626–634). Chichester, UK: John Wiley & Sons.

Jung, Y. (2010). Perception of (In)directness in Finnish and Korean Business Interaction. *The Journal of International Business Communication* 69, 9–16.

Jung, Y. (2017). *Professional Writing: A Discourse Analysis Approach*. Singapore: Cengage Learning.

Jung, Y. (2020). Empathy talk in call center. *ESP Review*, 2(2), 27–38.

Kasiri, L.A., Cheng, K.T.G., Sambasivan, M., & Sidin, S.M. (2017). Integration of standardization and customization: Impact on service quality, customer satisfaction, and loyalty. *Journal of Retailing and Consumer Services*, 35, 91–97.

Koester, A. (2004). Relational sequence in workplace genres, *Journal of Pragmatics*, 36, 1405–28.

Koester, A. (2006). *Investigating Workplace Discourse*. Abingdon: Routledge.

Koester, A. (2010). *Workplace Discourse*. London: Continuum.

Levinson, S. (1983). *Pragmatics.* Cambridge: Cambridge University Press.

McCarthy, M. (1998). *Spoken Language and Applied Linguistics*, Cambridge: Cambridge University Press.

McCarthy, M. (2000). Captive audiences: Small talk and close contact service encounters. In J. Coupland (Ed.) *Small Talk* (pp. 84–109). Harlow: Pearson Education.

Mirivel, J.C., & Tracy, K. (2005). Premeeting talk: An organizationally crucial form of talk. *Research on Language and Social Interaction*, 38(1), 1–34.

Nystrand, M. (1987). Framework. *International Journal of Business Communication*, 54(2), 182–198.

Pomerantz, A. (1984). Agreeing and disagreeing with assessments: some features of preferred/ dispreferred turn shapes. In J.M. Atkinson & J. Herritage (Eds.) *Structures of Social Action Studies in Conversation Analysis* (pp. 57–101). Cambridge: Cambridge University Press.

Spencer-Oatey, H. (2008). *Culturally Speaking: Managing Rapport through Talk Across Cultures* (2nd ed.). London: Continuum.

Swales, J.M. (1990). *Genre Analysis: English in Academic and Research Settings*. Cambridge: Cambridge University Press.

Traverso, V. (2001). Syrian service encounters: A case study of shifting strategies within verbal exchange. *Pragmatics*, 11(4), 421–444.

Ventola, E. (1987). *The Structure of Social Interaction: A systematic Approach to the Semiotics of Service Encounters*. London: Frances Pinter.

6 Korean business apology

6.1 Fundamental feature of business apology

Business organizations have face, which is public self-image (Jung 2017), like people. If they lose their face, they have an inclination to restore it. The threat of damaged reputation requires organizations to engage with the concept of reputation repair to restore the face of the organization by presenting a convincing account of organizational actions that are persuasive and legitimate (Argenti 2008). Organizations losing their face organize image repair strategies, and the dialogue between the organization and its publics after the negative occurrence is designed to minimize damage to the image of the organization. Restoring the image may be an effort to 'restoring the confidence of key publics, which means communicating a return to normal business' (Fearn-Banks 2002: 12). This is the fundamental idea for the theory of image restoration (Benoit 1995; Benoit and Czerwinski 1997; Benoit and Drew 1997). The fullest form of the image restoration strategies may come from Benoit's work (Benoit 1995, Benoit & Czerwinski 1997) articulated through image repair theory, which focuses on what a firm says when faced with a crisis. A distinction can generally be made between an avoidance statement (statement to avoid responsibility for a negative event) and an accommodative statement (statement to admit responsibility for a negative event) in the theory. Coombs (2007) adopts the concepts of locus and controllability to illustrate how people identify the cause of a crisis and decide where to place responsibility for the crisis when a negative and unpredictable event occurs. Locus refers to whether the cause of a crisis is internal or external to the organization. Controllability refers to whether the cause of a crisis is intentional or unintentional (Coombs 1995). Scholars have pointed out that the two causal dimensions of controllability and locus are indistinct in their operationalization and do not separately influence crisis outcomes (Lee 2004; McDonald et al. 2010; Moon and Rhee 2012). There are certain cases where two causal dimensions of controllability and locus are distinct. For example, a

DOI: 10.4324/9781003108061-6

dimension of external and intentional causes is the case of personal information leakage due to hacking damage or system overload caused by congestion in service use. A dimension of internal and unintentional causes is the case of the error in sending guidance email. On the way around, the causal dimensions of controllability and locus are not distinct depending on the cases. For instance, without a proper or understandable reason for food recall, the dimension is unclear. Or even with an acceptable reason for providing a poor service (e.g., franchise store's fault), it is not clear-cut if the dimension links to intentional or unintentional. This chapter dealing with both causal dimensions of controllability and locus supports the claim that selecting an effective crisis message for the given type of crisis is critical to reducing negative public responses (Coombs 2006; Moon and Rhee 2012). Special attention is paid to the accommodative statement admitting the wrongdoer's fault (exclusively an apology), in that an (authentic) apology is the most effective crisis message strategy among the many such strategies (Benoit and Drew 1997). Unlike pseudo-apology for mitigating the force of certain face-threats, an authentic apology can be made to neutralize the argumentative force of the initial charges of organizational wrongdoing (Jung 2014). An apology can marginally be classified into an explicit apology (clear/direct admittance of own responsibility for the failing event) and an implicit apology (unclear/indirect admittance of own responsibility for the failing event) (Moon and Lee 2012). Different conceptualizations of apology include other components, such as expressions of sympathy, provision of compensation, and a promise of corrective action (Patel and Reinsch 2003). In the letter of apology, an apology is made normally when we are at fault. In other words, no (explicit) apology is necessary when we are not at fault. It is because the phrases for apologies are generally interpreted to mean the sorry person is accepting blame or responsibility. An apology can be interpreted as an acknowledgment of the agent's or his or her organization's fault in causing trouble, so the extent of the problem can possibly appear serious to the victim(s). In this respect, an apology can contain various sets of components that determine its different definitions. Although this chapter is mainly about (explicit) apology as a type of corporate image restoration strategies, it also deals with implicit apology and discoursal elements more than an apology for corporate image restoration. This chapter exemplifies the claim that the proper understanding of the nature of accusation is a key to image repair discourse. This claim illustrates that attention has to be paid to the perlocutionary force, communication effect on how the message is recognized and perceived by the audience, for proper complaint management. Accordingly, it attempts to emphasize reader orientation in apologetic communication. The relative nature of communication behaviors for image restoration in complaint management situations will be discussed using the notion of *senguy* (성의, 'sincerity'). The way of showing *senguy* in apology is investigated with the length of the apologetic message, promise of a face-to-face apology, repetition of apology, and acknowledgment of headquarters' responsibility. To a lesser extent, the communication strategy of giving overwhelming reasons for wrongdoing is also explored to see if its function is to admit the organization's fault in the letter of Korean business apology. Before a discussion about all these, let us first investigate a genre-specific feature of the letter of Korean business apology.

6.2 Passive interaction genre

The letter of apology is, to some extent, a self-oriented or rather one-way communication genre. In one-way communication, a sender delivers a message to a receiver, but nothing flows back to the sender. Sometimes, one-way communication occurs because of the medium or method of communication. When we read a book, newspaper, or website, we play the part of the receiver in one-way communication. In these cases, the information moves in one direction because time and space separate the sender and the receiver. Print is a one-way communication medium. In general, to inform is a common purpose for one-way communication. The exchange may or may not occur after the fact. Consequently, the medium of communication and communication purpose influence the choice or type of information flow. The letter of apology is inherently a one-way communication genre. It is because a letter of apology is mainly distributed in newspapers, magazines, homepages, or emails, where the data from the chapter are also collected. The following two examples are emails notifying victims of the company's wrongdoing (*Leythe swusinkepwu/hoywenthalthoylul han hoywennimkkeyto OOsinmwun nyusuleytheka palsong* [레터 수신거부/회원탈퇴를 한 회원님께도 ○○신문 뉴스레터가 발송], 'OO Newspaper newsletter sent even to members who refuse to receive the letter or withdraw from membership', in example 9; *annaymeyili sisutheymcek olyulo inhay cwungpok palsong* [안내메일이 시스템적 오류로 인해 중복 발송], 'Duplicate sending of information mail due to system error', in example 10).

Example 9

Unit	Korean text	English translation
1	지난 1월 13일부터 18 일까지 레터수신거부/회 원탈퇴를한회원님들께도 OO신문뉴스레터가발송됐습니다.	The OO Newspaper newsletter was also sent from January 13 to 18 to members who refuse to receive or withdraw from their membership.

Unit	Korean text	English translation
2	회원 인증서버와 메일 발송 서버간의 연결 장애로 인해, 이 기간동안 변경된 회원정보가 제대로 반영이 되지 못해 일어난 일입니다.	This occurred because the member information changed during this period was not properly reflected due to a connection failure between the member authentication server and the mail-sending server.
3	회원님들께 불편을 드려 진심으로 사과 드립니다.	We sincerely apologize for the inconvenience to our members.
4	이러한 문제가 발생되지 않도록 더욱 노력하는 OO신문이 되겠습니다.	We, OO Newspaper, will work harder to prevent such problems.

Example 10

Unit	Korean text	English translation
1	안녕하세요? OO문고입니다.	Hello? This is OO Bookstore.
2	우선 고객님께 불편을 드려 죄송합니다.	First of all, we apologize for the inconvenience to our customers.
3	7월 1일 회원제도 변경에 관한 안내메일이시스템적오류로인 해중복발송 되었습니다.	On July 1, the information mail about the change in the membership system was sent due to a system error.
4	고객님은 7월 2일 수령하신 이메일상의 일반회원이 아닌 플래티넘 회원이십니다.	You are a platinum member, not a general member as stated in the email you received on July 2.
5	회원등급 반영에는 이상이 없으며 안내메일이 잘못 발송된 것임을 거듭 말씀드립니다.	We reiterate that there is no problem with your membership level and that the information email was sent incorrectly.
6	다시 한 번 고객님께 불편을 드린 점 깊이 사과드립니다.	Once again, we deeply apologize for any inconvenience caused to our customers.
7	앞으로 더욱 노력하는 OO 문고가 되겠습니다.	In the future, we, OO Bookstore, will make more of an effort.

These examples do not use a language device linking the present event to the future event at the very end of each example, such as *Caceyhan nayyongun cenhwa OOlo mwunuyhasiki palapnita* (자세한 내용은 전화 OO로 문의하시기 바랍니다, 'Please call us at OO for more detail'). The writers do not show anticipation of future correspondence after completing a present event, an apology for his company's wrongdoing. This illustrates that the letter of apology is, to some extent, a self-oriented or rather one-way communication genre. In this respect, the letter of apology violates good practices of business writing. Good organizational writing does not begin with an assertive act (what the writer thinks about his or her subject), but an act of listening (what others think). Writing well means engaging the voices of others. Accordingly, writing is a 'conversational' act (Graff and Birkenstein 2010). In business writing, a writer not only wants his or her words to be understood (an illocutionary effect in speech-act terms), but also to be accepted (a perlocutionary effect or reader action). This claim raises the issue of the relative or relational nature of communicative phenomena for business success. The reciprocal or dynamic nature of business communication suggests that the writer takes the reader's needs into account when producing discourse. It goes along well with *you*-attitude, the reciprocal or dynamic nature of communication. *You*-attitude is a communication style that looks at phenomena from the audience's perspective (Jung 2014, 2017; Locker et al. 2018). It considers how the message is recognized and perceived by the audience, as opposed to the actual content of the message realized by the writer. The deficiency of the reciprocal or dynamic nature of communication in the letter of a Korean business apology can be supplemented by the techniques to show *senguy* (성의), the maxim of sincerity. Since sufficient degree of *senguy* might be one of the victims' major expectations in the letter of apology, it would raise the possibility of forgiving the accused's wrongdoing. The next section explores methods to express *senguy* in Korean business apology.

6.3   Showing *senguy* in the letter of apology

An apology serves to protect an organization's reputation after a business crisis when its publics view the organization as responsible for the crisis (Coombs and Holladay 1996). An apology from a company raised consumers' satisfaction and the perceived fairness or responses when service failures were involved (Goodwin and Ross 1992). If an apology is not delivered in a crisis situation, it may be seen as defensive or inadequate in the eyes of the organization's publics. An apology actively admitting crisis responsibility contributes to relieving public anger in a crisis situation (Lee and Chung 2012). If a company is in the situation of making an apology, it might be better to do it early with a correction of the situation. Despite the advantages of an apology in protecting corporate reputations, Choi and Lin (2009) maintain that the value of an apology has been questioned. The following example may exemplify the claim that proper corporate image restoration demands more than an (explicit) apology. It is a letter of apology for sending invitation letters for a fan signature meeting to the wrong audiences.

Example 11

Unit	Korean text	English translation
1	2월 7일 (금) 예정된 OO 팬사인회 관련하여 잘못 안내된 부분에 대한 내용 정정 및 사과의 말씀드립니다.	We would like to apologize and correct the contents of the incorrect information regarding the OO fan signing event scheduled for February 7 (Friday).
2	2월 4일 (화) 오후 8시 팬사인회 당첨자 100명 외에 내부적으로 불참을 대비해 선정한 예비당첨자에게도 당첨 이메일 및 푸시 메시지 안내가 나가는 오류가 있었습니다. 추가 명단은 신종 코로나바이러스 감염증 우려로 인하여, 일부 당첨자의 행사 불참을 대비해 마련한 명단입니다.	In addition to the 100 winners of the fan signing event at 8 p.m. on Tuesday, February 4, there was an error in the winning e-mail and push message sent out to preliminary winners who were internally selected in anticipation of dropouts. The additional list was prepared in case some winners were unable to attend the event due to concerns about the novel coronavirus [Covid-19] infection.
3	최초 당첨자 명단은 기존에 공지해 드린 명단 (100명) 입니다. 추가로 이메일 및 푸시 메시지로만 당첨 안내를 받으신 분들께서는 죄송한 말씀이오나 팬사인회 참석이 어렵습니다.	The first winner list is the previously announced list (100 people). In addition, we are sorry, but those who received the winning announcement only by email and push message cannot be allowed to attend the fan signing event.
4	많은 기대를 하셨을 고객님께 혼선을 드린 점 진심으로 사과드립니다.	We sincerely apologize for the confusion to our customers who expected more.

Apologies focusing on accepting responsibility are more likely to be accepted by various publics than denial, excuses, or justification when an organization is responsible for a crisis (Kim et al. 2009). When an organization accepts more responsibility after a transgression, its publics feel less anger toward the organization (Pace et al. 2010). An apology focusing on accepting responsibility results in less reputation damage than rejecting responsibility. Nevertheless, the wrongdoer's simple apology may look something short of curing the victim's injuries. Although apologies play a role in neutralizing the argumentative force of the charges of organizational wrongdoing in principle, it is not sure if apologies themselves are good enough to sympathize with fans moving heaven and hell in example 11. Publics tend to perceive the organization in a more positive way up to the level of sincerity in accepting the responsibility the organization takes for a crisis. Let us extend the discussion about this claim with the label of *senguy* ('sincerity') for now.

6.3.1 *Length of the letter of apology*

Since written business communication is a goal-oriented activity, a direct tone can be used for maximum efficiency by letting the reader know the urgency based on mutually shared knowledge (see Jung 2014, 2017 for the maxim of clarity in business writing). Good business writing practices can be mostly done in a clear or short style. Clarity is the most highly valued element in business writing, and it is the primary goal for most writing in business. A clear tone can be realized by simple message structures (i.e., simple paragraphing, short sentences). Naturally, simple paragraphs and short messages can make texts relatively clear and obvious. To give too much information in a simple sentence/paragraph is to risk falling short of the communication purpose of the text, as explained by Ries and Trout's (2000) argument that the problem of over-communication can be attributed to the limited mental capacities of audiences. A simple message with a short paragraph structure may lessen the audience's time and energy used for interpretation, so the core intent of the message should not be unclear. Simple paragraphs, short messages, and familiar words for both ends (e.g., the language that most of us use in daily conversation) can make texts relatively clear and obvious. For the sentence level, audiences in business settings tend to prefer brief and simple sentences over long, complex ones. To give too much information in a single sentence/paragraph is to risk obscuring the communication purpose of the text. Given the claim, it is noteworthy that the following letter of apology observes the short style in order to make a clear apology message (e.g., simple/short paragraphing: a reason for apology [unit 1], corrective action [unit 2], and an apology [unit 3]). It is the case of a system error setting a wrong price.

Example 12

Unit	Korean text	English translation
1	5월 24일 새벽 0시 – 4시 30분 사이 발생한 가격오기는 사이트 개편 후 안정화 기간 중 일어난 시스템 오류입니다.	The price error that occurred between 0:00 a.m. and 4:30 a.m. on May 24 is a system error that occurred during the stabilization period after the online site reorganization.

Unit	Korean text	English translation
2	해당 주문에 대한 처리는 고객님들께 전화와 메일로 안내해드릴 예정입니다.	Customers will be notified of the processing of the order by phone and email.
3	다시 한번 이용에 불편을 드려 대단히 죄송합니다.	Once again, we are very sorry for the inconvenience.

On the way around, a message length is likely to be an essential convention for showing sincerity in the letter of business and/or professional apology. Message structures and length become complex and longer to meet the requirement of sincerity for the letter of business apology. Short/simple messages for an apology may wrongly convey that the company does not take its wrongdoing seriously, as a (too) short and/or simple message may look careless or insincere. Example 13 comes across as being more sincere than example 12 because of the complexity of its paragraph structure: apology (unit 1), reason for apology (unit 2), giving compensation (unit 3), corrective action (unit 4), and apology (unit 5). It is a letter of apology for a food safety problem published in a newspaper. Selecting either a simple or complex paragraph structure is influenced by the size or degree of seriousness of the company's wrongdoing (e.g., wrong price setting error in example 12 vs. food recall in example 13). Different cases of wrongdoing may make the apologizer decide which type of paragraph structure for an apology. Nevertheless, it is certain that a complex paragraph structure is likely to enhance the perception of sincerity in a written apology.

Example 13

Unit	Korean text	English translation
1	당사 xx 제품 건으로 고객 여러분께 심려를 끼쳐드린 점에 대해 진심으로 사과드립니다.	We sincerely apologize for causing concern to our customers with our xx products.
2	당사는 2016년 5월 15일 생산한 xx 제품에 대해 정부의 수거검사 결과 세균발육시험에서 양성판정 및 회수를 통보받았습니다.	As a result of the government's collection test for xx products produced on May 15, 2016, we were informed of the positive determination of bacterial growth.
3	이에 따라, 가정내에 보관하고 계신 해당 제품은 전량 환불이 가능합니다. 또한, 고객 불안 해소를 위해 해당 제품 외 당사의 유사 제품에 대해서도 원하실 경우 환불해 드리겠습니다.	Accordingly, the entire cost of the product can be refunded. In addition, to relieve customer anxiety, we will refund similar products other than the corresponding product.

(*Continued*)

Unit	Korean text	English translation
4	이번에 문제가 된 제품에 대해 정확한 원인을 규명하도록 최선을 다하겠습니다. 아울러 ○○제품의 원인규명 및 안정성 확보시까지 당사 관련 전 제품의 잠정적 생산 및 판매중지를 통해 고객 불만을 최소화할 수 있도록 하겠습니다. 이번 일을 계기로 ○○주식회사 임직원 일동은 식품안전에 더욱 만전을 기해 고객 여러분들의 기대와 성원에 보답하도록 노력하겠습니다.	We will do our best to determine the exact cause of contamination in the product in question. In addition, we will address customer complaints by temporarily suspending production and sales of all products related to our company until the cause of the OO product is identified and its stability is secured. Taking this opportunity, all the executives and employees of OO Co. Ltd. will strive to meet customers' expectations and support by being more thorough in our food safety.
5	다시 한 번 고객 여러분께 진심으로 사과드립니다.	Once again, we sincerely apologize to our customers.

6.3.2   *Promise of a face-to-face apology*

Media have the ability to transmit needed information. This ability to transmit depends on whether the information will be used in times of uncertainty or equivocality (Daft and Lengel 1986). According to Daft and Lengel (1986), the need for a communication task is sometimes necessary to reduce uncertainty (involves finding the right answer for a question) or to reduce equivocality (finding the right question to answer). For example, lean media (emails) is best used to reduce uncertainty, and rich media (face-to-face) is best suited for reducing equivocality. There are few criteria judging the richness of media. Every media has different levels of personal focus; especially when a media incorporates more personal feelings and emotions, the message gets conveyed fully in better terms (e.g., communicating face-to-face as compared to communication via email). 'Rich media' refers to media that allows users to quickly respond to the communication that is being received. The medium should be able to support two-way communication. Media can be ranked in the following descending order in terms of their richness: face-to-face, video systems, audio systems, and text systems. In conclusion, it can be stated that different communication methods of media should be used based on their levels of richness. Example 14 exemplifies that the (promise of) a face-to-face apology makes the apologizer appear to be the most formal and sincere, including the letter of apology. In the following example, OO Hotel damages a customer's car during a hotel staff's valet parking.

Example 14

Unit	Korean text	English translation
1	○○호텔 고객관리를 담당하는 총 책임자 ○○○입니다.	I am OO, in charge of hotel customer management.
2	먼저, ○○호텔을 대표하여 ○○회사 ○○○이사님의 차량에 발생한 문제에 대해 심심한 사과의 말씀을 전합니다.	First of all, on behalf of OO Hotel, I would like to express my sincere apology for the problem that occurred.
3	저희 ○○호텔은 고객님들에게 최고의 서비스를 제공하는 것을 목표로 삼고 항상 최선을 다하고 있으나, 직원들의 부주의로 인해 이러한 일이 발생하게 되어 대단히 송구합니다.	We, OO Hotel, aim to provide the best service to our customers and are always doing our best, and we are very sorry that this happened due to the carelessness of our staff.
4	저희 측에서는 해당 직원들을 엄중히 문책하고, 그에 맞는 징계 처분을 내렸습니다.	On our end, we severely reprimanded the employees, and took appropriate disciplinary actions.
5	저희 ○○호텔에서는 이에 보상하는 차원에서 손상된 차량의 수리비용을 일체 부담할 것이며, 진심으로 사과하는 뜻에서 저희 호텔 숙박권을 보내드리기로 결정하였습니다.	In order to compensate you for this, we, OO Hotel, will bear the entire cost of repairing the damaged vehicle, and we will also send you a hotel voucher as a token of our sincere apology.
6	비록 작은 사과의 표시이지만, 이로 인해 ○○○이사님의 노여움이 조금이라도 풀어지시길 바랍니다.	Although it is a token of a small apology, we hope that this will alleviate your anger.
7	저희 ○○호텔은 이번 일을 계기로 하여 다시는 불미스러운 일이 발생하지 않도록 최선을 다해 노력하겠습니다.	We, OO Hotel, will do our best to prevent anything unpleasant from happening again.
8	거듭 사과의 말씀을 전하며, 조만간 찾아뵙고 정식으로 사과 드리겠습니다.	We apologize again, and we will see you soon and formally apologize.

Alongside numerous explicit apologies (*sakwauy malssum* [사과의 말씀], 'words of apology'; *taytanhi songkwuhapnita* [대단히 송구합니다], 'I am very sorry'; *ketupsakwa* [거듭사과], 'repeated apology'), corrective actions are made which reflect that the hotel is taking the situation seriously in terms of fully admitting OO Hotel's fault and by punishing the wrongdoers (*haytang cikwentulul mwunchaykkwa cingkyey* [해당 직원들을 문책과 징계], 'reprimand and discipline those employees'). Showing their willingness to offer a tangible or intangible compensation is another way to make a convincing apology. Compensation refers to forms of financial returns and tangible services and benefits that stakeholders receive as part of a stakeholder's relationships (Milkovich and Newman 2005). The main benefits of offering compensation are ways of solving the problem. By expressing its willingness to provide compensation, the company seems to be sincerely attempting to ressolve this problem. In this respect, OO Hotel promises to offer compensation to the victim (*chalyang swulipiyong* [차량 수리비용], 'vehicle repair cost'; *hotheyl swukpakkwen* [호텔 숙박권], 'hotel voucher'). Although example 14 is full of such statements admitting OO Hotel's fault, the apologizer, a general manager from the hotel, may think that using email is too informal hence insincere. Accordingly, he promises to make a 'formal' apology, this being a face-to-face apology (as described in unit 8: *Comankan chatapoypko cengsikulo sakwa tulikeysssupnita* [조만간 찾아뵙고 정식으로 사과 드리겠습니다], 'We'll see you soon and formally apologize'). The choice of rich media for an apology may help interpersonal communication become more like two-way communication in that there is an added advantage for a face-to-face apology (e.g., to reduce the equivocality by observing the addressee's body languages, including facial expressions).

6.3.3 Acknowledgment of headquarters' responsibility

Korean business practices and customs are deeply influenced by cultural values. For example, the nature of the hierarchical order is the underlying cause of the predominantly vertical nature of the relationships in Korean business organizations. The collectivistic nature of Korean society causes strong family ties to be extended to the work environment so that the work organization can function very much like a family (Jung 2009). A parent company (*kulup* [그룹], 'conglomerate') is responsible for its subsidiaries (*cahoysa* [자회사]). A sincere apology made by the parent company may generally be a proper and efficient method of image restoration to show 'responsible leadership' (Baum 2006). A company at fault is most persuasive when it admits that fault and when apologies are exclusively from the parent company or headquarters. In this respect, the following two apology messages show sincerity in apology in that the headquarters/franchiser (*ponpwu/ponsa* [본부/본사]) is willing to acknowledge its responsibility for wrongdoing (e.g., *kokaykseynthe cikwen kyoyuk mit kwanliey sohol-haeyssten ponpwuey chaykim* [고객센터 직원 교육 및 관리에 소홀하였던 본부에 책임], 'responsibility for the headquarters that neglected to train and manage customer center staff', in example 15; *ponsaey chaykimi isstanun kesul thongkam* [본사에 책임이 있다는 것을 통감], 'realizing that the head office is responsible', in example 16).

Example 15

Unit	Korean text	English translation
1	○○푸드 주식회사 ○○입니다.	This is OO from OO Food Co. Ltd.
2	먼저 진심 어린 사과의 말씀 드립니다.	First of all, I would like to express my sincere apology.
3	○○푸드 가맹점과 고객센터의 미숙한 응대로 인해 저희 브랜드를 사랑해 주시는 고객님들께 불편함을 끼쳐 드렸습니다.	Due to the inexperienced response of the OO Food franchise store and customer center, we have caused inconvenience to customers who love our brand.
4	가맹점 관리뿐만 아니라 <u>고객센터 직원 교육 및 관리에 소홀하였던 본부에</u> 책임이 있다는 것을 통감하고 고객님들께 깊은 사과를 드립니다.	We deeply apologize to our customers, knowing that the headquarters is responsible for not only managing franchise stores but also neglecting to train and manage customer center staff.
5	우선적으로 고객님께는 본부와 해당 가맹점 점주님이 직접 사과를 할 수 있도록 하고, 해당 가맹점은 일주일간 영업을 중단하고 서비스 교육을 진행하도록 하겠습니다. 이후 해당 가맹점의 잘못된 응대로 피해를 입으신 고객님의 불편사항을 전 가맹점주 및 직원들과 함께 공유하고 차후 동일한 불만사항이 발생하지 않도록 전 가맹점을 대상으로 체계적인 서비스 교육을 실시하겠습니다.	First of all, we will let the headquarters and the affiliated store owners apologize directly to the customer, and the franchise store will be suspended for one week, and service training will be conducted. After that, we will share the complaints of customers who have suffered damage due to the wrong response of the franchise store with all franchisees and employees and conduct systematic service training for all franchisees to prevent the same problems from occurring in the future.

Example 16

Unit	Korean text	English translation
1	본사 가족점과 관련해 문의 주신 고객님의 글을 확인하였습니다.	We checked your mail that inquired about the franchise store.

(Continued)

Unit	Korean text	English translation
2	이에 즉시 본사 담당자가 해당 가맹점에서의 경위를 파악하고 금일 1차 서비스 교육 및 경고 조치를 진행했습니다.	After this, the head office personnel immediately grasped the circumstances of the franchise store and conducted the first service training and warning measures today.
3	그리고 이 모든 일들은 가족점 관리에 소홀하였던 본사에 책임이 있다는것을 통감하고 고객님들께 깊은 사과를 드립니다.	And we deeply apologize to our customers, knowing that the head office has been responsible for all these matters for neglecting to manage the franchise store.
4	아울러 (주)○○푸드의 대표이사 및 임직원 일동은 피해 고객님께 다시 한번 사과의 말씀을 전하며, 한 가족점 뿐만 아니라 전국 270개 ○○ 푸드 가족점에 대한 공식적인 서비스 점검과 함께 재발 방지를 약속 드립니다.	The CEO and all of the staff of OO Food Co. Ltd once again apologize to the customer and promise to prevent recurrence with official service checks not only for one franchise store but also for 270 franchise stores nationwide.

6.3.4   Repetition of apology

Repetition can go by a negative label, the so-called name of redundancy. Namely, the repetition of old information may violate the maxim of brevity, so it may make the text less clear and not coherent. However, the use of repetition can support the claim that clarity does not always call for brevity. For example, the function of repetition is to boost sincerity, which is a hallmark of the Korean business apology text. An apology is repeated three times (*cinsimulo sakwatulipnita* [진심으로 사과드립니다], 'I sincerely apologize' in unit 1; *kiphun sacoyuy malssum* [깊은 사죄의 말씀], 'a deep apology' in unit 2; *cinsimulo coysonghan maum* [진심으로 죄송한 마음], 'sincerely sorry' in unit 3; *tasi han pen sakwa tulipnita* [다시 한 번 사과 드립니다], 'I apologize once again' in unit 4) in the following example, the letter of apology printed in the company's website for an error in the online reservation system of OO Cinema.

Example 17

Unit	Korean text	English translation
1	○○ 시네마를 애용하여 주시는 고객님께, 홈페이지 이용에 불편을 드린 점 진심으로사과드립니다.	We sincerely apologize for any inconvenience caused to customers who have used OO Cinema's website.

Unit	Korean text	English translation
2	성탄절을 맞이하여 OO 시네마/ 예매서비스 이용이 많아짐에 따라 홈페이지 서비스 이용에 불편을 드리게 되었습니다. <u>깊은사죄의말씀</u>을 드립니다.	In the Christmas season, as the use of OO Cinema reservation service increased, it made customers inconvenient in using the website service. I would like to express my deep apology.
3	편리한 서비스를 제공하여 드리고자 노력하였으나 예기치 못한 상황으로 불편함을 드리게 되어 <u>진심으로죄송한마음</u> 뿐입니다.	We have tried to provide convenient services, but we are truly sorry for any inconvenience caused by unexpected circumstances.
4	보다 안정적이고 편리한 서비스를 제공하여 드릴 수 있도록 더욱 더 노력하는 OO 시네마가 되겠습니다. 고객님의 많은 양해 부탁 드리며, 불편을 드린 점 <u>다시한번사과드립니다</u>.	We will make more efforts to provide more stable and convenient services. We ask for your understanding and apologize again for any inconvenience caused.

Repetition comes up in a positive sense in example 17. We can have a positive label for repetition when it has a certain purpose (a positive sense, exclusively). Example 17 illustrates that although clarity is a goal for standard business writing and it calls for brevity in principle, this claim cannot be equally applicable, depending on the situation. Repetition can be used in order to deliver the key information, an apology, in a clear, coherent, and sincere manner. The repetition of apology is also to express sympathy. Sympathy focuses on expressing the organization's sincere sorrow and concern for those affected by a crisis to stimulate positive public emotions toward the organization (Moon and Rhee 2012). Demonstrating sympathy can help shape public perceptions of an organization positively or less negatively (Coombs and Holladay 2007). Coombs and Holladay (2007) show that there is no significant difference between the effect of accepting responsibility and expressing sympathy on public responses when an organization has a moderate level of responsibility for causing a crisis. Since sympathies indicate a high level of accommodation in a crisis situation through the focus on victims' needs (Sturges 1994), the strategic value of expressions of sympathy helps increase the perceived sincerity of the statement (Weiner 1986).

6.4 Giving a reason for wrongdoing

One of the strongest applications of shared knowledge is to establish a common ground with the reader. If the writer initially expresses opinions held in common with the reader, he or she will be more likely to change the readers' opinions or perceptions on other issues. By claiming a common ground, therefore, the writer can increase his or her chance of persuading the reader of his or her main point. As Limaye (1997: 38) observes, the presence of an explanation is a moral issue, insisting on the moral obligation of writers to provide an explanation, arguing that offering the reader both general and specific reasons is not an option but an 'ethical imperative'. Johnson and Indvik (2002) research a similar conclusion that the value of presenting a reasoned explanation is seen as a contribution to a positive or less negative interpretation of the negative news. They also emphasize that explanations indicating external environmental factors as the cause of the negative news are perceived more positively by the reader than those linking the negative news to an action taken by the recipient. Given the claim, the writer needs to provide sufficient evidence, statistics, data, and other material credible to the reader. As supportive statements, plausible reasons are 'external modifications' because they modify the force of the negative message within their immediate context without being placed within a negative message (Faerch and Kasper 1989). When supportive reasons given by the writer are understandable and reasonable to the reader, they act as mitigators. Therefore, in informing the reader of negative news, the action can be assessed for its underlying motive. In this respect, proposing proper and overwhelming reasons for giving negative news seems productive and reasonable to mitigate the force of the negative news. The writer can also save his own face by justifying his unavoidable wrongdoing through his explicit explanation of difficult situations incurring the mistake or fault. If a delay or problem is due to circumstances beyond the accused's control, it may be appropriate to include an explanation so that the reader knows he was not negligent. Coombs (2007) claims that people identify the cause/reason of a crisis and decide where to place responsibility for the crisis when a negative and unpredictable event occurs. The various publics' causal attributions affect the way people view a company, which can seriously affect the organization's reputation (Coombs and Holladay 2007). Anger is strongly elicited when consumers attribute the cause of a crisis to a company. It is affected by how much publics believe a crisis is caused by internal factors or an organization (Coombs 2007). According to Lee (2004), people who perceive that the crisis responsibility is within the boundaries of an organization (i.e., internal locus) are likely to regard the crisis as controllable, whereas those who perceive that the crisis responsibility is outside the realm of an organization (i.e., external locus) are likely to view it as uncontrollable. If an organization is judged to have been in a controllable negative event, anger is evoked, whereas if the organization is judged not to have been able to control a crisis, pity is elicited (Coombs and Holladay 2007; Hareli and Weiner 2002). Namely, people who think a crisis is caused by internal factors of an organization attribute more crisis responsibility to the organization than those who think a crisis is caused by an external factor (Lee 2004). People who think a crisis is caused by external factors in an organization have less negative responses to a business apology. External factors might generate less negative public responses (Nadler and Liviatan 2006). This claim is exemplified by the following four examples, cases of private information leakage.

Example 18

Korean text	English translation
이번 사고 경위는 2013년 6월 저희 회사의 카드부정사용방지시스템을 고도화하는 과정에서 개발을 맡았던 개인신용정보회사의개발담당책임자가 불법으로 고객 정보를 절취하여 반출시킨 것입니다.	In June 2013, in the process of upgrading our company's card fraud prevention system, <u>the person in charge of the development of a personal credit information company</u> illegally stole customer information and removed it.

Example 19

Korean text	English translation
경찰은_불법적인_목적으로_ 지난해_2월부터_최근까지_당사의_ 홈페이지에서_고객님의_개인정보를_ 유출시킨 범인을_검거했다고_ 발표하였습니다.	The police announced that they had arrested <u>the criminal who leaked your personal information</u> on our website from February last year until recently for illegal purposes.

Example 20

Korean text	English translation
폐사의 건강잡지 구독신청 웹 페이지는 2016년 5월 14일 경 <u>중국발로추정되는 IP</u>로 부터 해킹 피해를 당하였고, 그 결과 2010 년 4월부터 2016년 5월 14일까지 사이에 해당 웹 페이지를 통해 건강 잡지를 신청하셨던 약 2만 8천여 명의 고객님의 이름, 아이디, 연락처, 이메일 및 주소가 유출된 것으로 파악이 되었습니다.	Our health magazine subscription web page was hacked from <u>an IP estimated to originate from China</u> around May 14, 2016, and as a result, through the web page from April 2010 to May 14, 2016. It was found that the names, IDs, contact details, email addresses, and addresses of about 28,000 customers who applied for health magazines were leaked.

Example 21

Korean text	English translation
저희 ○○영어는 고객님의 개인정보 보호에 최우선으로 노력해 왔으나, 최근 교육업계를 대상으로 한 <u>악의적인 해커</u>의 소행에 의해 고객님의 개인정보가 침해되는 사고가 발생하였음을 알게 되었습니다.	We, OO English, have been making efforts to protect your personal information as a top priority, but we learned that an accident occurred in which your personal information was infringed by <u>malicious hackers</u> targeting the education industry.

The apologizers pinpoint wrongdoers (i.e., *kayin sinyongcengpohoysauy kaypaltamtangca* [개인신용정보회사의 개발담당자], 'a development manager of personal credit information company', in example 18; *kayin-cenpolul yuchwulsikhin pemin* [개인정보를 유출시킨 범인], 'the criminal who leaked personal information', in example 19; *cwungkwukpallo chwu-cengtoynun IP* [중국발로 추정되는 IP], 'an IP estimated from China', in example 20; *akuycekin haykhe* [해커], 'malicious hacker', in example 21). It is to deliver a message that wrongdoing is made by the third party, and the apologizer's company is also a victim. Accordingly, the crisis responsibility within the boundaries of an organization is unlikely.

Giving an overwhelming reason for giving unwelcome news may be loosely linked to Brown and Levinson's positive politeness in that if the supportive reason conveyed by the writer (e.g., hacking damage or accident) is also understandable and reasonable to the reader, this could easily bring about the reader's agreement. Nevertheless, seeking agreement on the writer's face-threatening act (FTA) may have nothing to do with the reader's positive face wants. Instead, it may only reflect the writer's positive face wants to invite sympathy from the reader. In a similar vein, if a reason does not seem appropriate to the reader, the reader does not accept the reason as a mitigating device. Instead, the reason possibly increases damage to the reader's positive face. A reason may double the damage to the reader's positive face, as the reason for wrongdoing itself is unwelcome news to the reader. In this respect, giving overwhelming reasons does not inherently function to mitigate the force of the FTAs. The following two examples published in local newspapers, cases of offering poor services from food franchise stores, support this claim in that the companies try to emphasize the undesirable external factor (*kamayngcem* [가맹점]), 'franchise store') as a reason for wrongdoing, offering a poor service.

Example 22

Unit	Korean text	English translation
1	지난 12월 15일 발생한 ○ ○점 <u>가맹점주</u>의 적절치 못한 고객 응대로 인해 피해를 입은 해당 고객님뿐 아니라 저희 ○ ○푸드를 애용해 주시는 많은 고객님들께 진심으로 사과의 말씀을 드립니다.	We sincerely apologize not only to the customers who have suffered damage from the OO franchise store owner's inappropriate customer response that occurred on December 15 but also to many customers who use OO Food.
2	해당 <u>가맹점</u> 점주는 현재 깊이 반성하고 있으며, 피해를 입은 고객님께 진심으로 사과의 말씀을 전하기 위해 최선을 다하고 있습니다.	The owner of the franchise store is very regretful and is trying his best to convey a sincere apology to the affected customers.
3	하지만 ○ ○푸드 본사는 절대 있어서는 안 될 비상식적 고객 응대로 일관한 해당 <u>가맹점</u>에 강력한 경고 조치와 함께 본사 차원의 영업 정지 후 <u>가맹점</u> 계약 해지를 검토 중에 있습니다.	However, the head office of OO Food is reviewing the termination of the contract with the franchise store after a suspension of business at the head office level, along with a strong warning measurement to the franchise store consistently in response to unconscious customer response that should never occur.
4	○ ○푸드는 이번 일과 관련하여 추후 같은 일이 다시는 반복되는 일이 없도록 최선을 다할 것을 약속드리며, 전 <u>가맹점</u>에 대한 고객 서비스 마인드도 재교육 할 예정입니다.	OO Food promises to do its best to ensure that the same thing will not be repeated in the future in connection with this work and plans to retrain customer service minds for all franchise stores.
5	○ ○푸드를 애용해 주시는 많은 고객분들께 다시 한번 고개 숙여 진심으로 사과의 말씀을 드립니다.	We sincerely apologize once again to many customers who love OO Food.

Example 23

Unit	Korean text	English translation
1	○ ○푸드의 모든 제품은 전 매장 동일한 레시피로 제조하며, 최상의 품질을 균일하게 제공하고자 노력하고 있습니다.	All products of OO Food are manufactured with the same recipe in all stores, and we are striving to provide the best quality uniformly.

(*Continued*)

Unit	Korean text	English translation
2	ㅇㅇ푸드는 7월 22일 한 가맹점 매장에서 ㅇㅇ제품에 대한 소비자 불만이 접수된 사실을 인지했습니다. 그 후, ㅇㅇ푸드는 해당 가맹점주와 논의해 환불 조치 진행하였습니다.	OO Food recognizes that on July 22, a consumer complained about an OO product at a franchise store. After that, we, OO Food, discussed [the issue] with the franchise store owner and proceeded with a refund.
3	이번 일로 인해 ㅇㅇ푸드를 사랑해 주시는 고객님들께 실망을 드려 진심으로 사과 드립니다.	We sincerely apologize for disappointment to the customers who love OO Food.
4	본사는 물론 가맹점 모두 이번 사안에 대해 심각성을 느끼고 있습니다. 이에 ㅇ ㅇ푸드 본사는 해당 매장에 즉각 제품 및 CS교육을 재실시하였습니다.	Both the head office and the franchise stores understand the seriousness of this issue. Accordingly, the OO Food headquarters immediately reconducted CS training at the store.
5	이번 일을 계기로 ㅇㅇ푸드는 제품 제조과정을 전반적으로 재점검하고, 다시는 이런 일이 재발하지 않도록 전 매장에 교육을 실시하겠습니다.	Taking this opportunity, OO Food will reexamine the product manufacturing process as a whole and provide training to all stores to prevent this from happening again.

Acknowledgments of the company's responsibility are apparently made (i.e., apologies: *sakwauy malssum* [사과의 말씀], 'words of apology', in example 22; *sakwa tulipnita* [사과 드립니다], 'apologize', in example 23). Also, the headquarters take corrective actions (*kamayngcemey kanglyekhan kyengko cochiwa yengepcengci* [가맹점에 강력한 경고 조치와 영업정지], 'strong warning measures and business suspension to franchisees'; *kamayngcem kyeyyak hayci* [가맹점 계약 해지], 'franchisee contract termination'; *kokayk sepisu maintu caykyoyuk* [고객 서비스 마인드 재교육], 'customer service mind retraining', in example 22; *hwanpwulcochi, ceyphwum mit CS kyoyuk caysilsi, ceycokwaceng caycemkem, cen maycangey kyoyuk silsi* [환불조치, 제품 및 CS 교육 재실시, 제조과정 재점검, 전 매장에 교육 실시], 'refunds, product and CS training reinspection, manufacturing process reinspection, training in all stores', in example 23). Although sincere apologies and corrective actions go hand in hand with efforts to rectify the problem, the messages state avoidance of accidental damage. A reason for wrongdoing (i.e., *kamayngcem/maycang*, 'franchise store') serves the function of shifting the blame from the company. It is an effort to save the corporate image by shifting the blame to a particular franchise store. Unlike simple denial of accusation, the apologizers try to shift the blame to the franchise store. This corresponds to Hearit's (1995) notion of 'scapegoating' (transfer guilt to another). Alongside apology and corrective actions, the use of the scapegoating strategy may support the claim that a variety of image restoration strategies in a single example exemplify that the theory of image restoration discourse tends to focus on types of strategies without an in-depth consideration of the harmonization between and among different strategies. The strategy of scapegoating makes us doubt how much the companies tend to admit their responsibilities for the problems. This seems to contradict the sincerity of apologies that acknowledge headquarters' responsibility (see section 6.3.3). Despite its inherently accommodation-oriented characteristic, the strategy of giving a reason for unwelcome news plays a role in the avoidance of the company's fault on this occasion. This may be supported by the claim that statements and actions avoiding a company's responsibility are less risky, as Coombs and Holladay (2007) reveal that when an organization delivers an apology admitting responsibility for a crisis, the organization potentially opens itself to lawsuits and the apology may be used as evidence in court to win lawsuits against the organization. Also, if people attribute a greater amount of crisis responsibility to an organization, they are likely to rate the organization more negatively (Coombs and Holladay 2002). Therefore, it is assumed that publics hold a negative impression and distrust a company when the company is obviously responsible for a crisis.

References

Argenti, P. (2008). *Corporate Communication* (5th ed.). Boston: McGraw-Hill/ Irwin.

Baum, H. (2006). *The transparent leader: how to build a great company through straight talk, openness, and accountability.* N.Y.: HarperCollins.

Benoit, W.L. (1995). *Accounts, Excuses, and Apologies: A Theory of Image Restoration Strategies.* Albany: State University of New York Press.

Benoit, W.L., & Czerwinski, A. (1997). A critical analysis of USAir's image repair discourse. *Business Communication Quarterly*, 60(3), 38–57.

Benoit, W.L., & Drew, S. (1997). Appropriateness and effectiveness of image repair strategies. *Communication Reports*, 10, 153–163.

Choi, Y., & Lin, Y-H. (2009). Consumer responses to Mattel product recalls posted on online bulletin boards: Exploring two types of emotion. *Journal of Public Relations Research*, 21, 198–207.

Coombs, W.T. (1995). Choosing the right words: The development of guidelines for the selection of the 'appropriate' crisis-response strategies. *Management Communication Quarterly*, 8, 447–476.

Coombs, W.T. (2006). The protective powers of crisis response strategies: Managing reputational assets during a crisis. *Journal of Promotion Management*, 12, 241–259.

Coombs, W.T. (2007). Protecting organization reputations during a crisis: The development and application of situational crisis communication theory. *Corporate Reputation Review*, 10, 163–176.

Coombs, W.T., & Holladay, S.J. (1996). Communication and attributions in a crisis: An experimental study in crisis communication. *Journal of Public Relations Research*, 8, 279–295.

Coombs, W.T., & Holladay, S.J. (2002). Helping crisis managers protect reputational assets: Initial tests of the situational crisis communication theory. *Management Communication Quarterly*, 16, 165–186.

Coombs, W.T., & Holladay, S.J. (2007). Comparing apology to equivalent crisis response strategies: Clarifying apology's role and value in crisis communication. *Public Relations Review*, *34*, 252–257.

Daft, R.L., & Lengel, R.H. (1986). Organizational information requirement, media richness and structural design. *Management Science*, 32, 554–571.

Faerch, C., & Kasper, G. (1989). Internal and external modification in interlanguage request realization. In S. Blum-Kulka, J. House, & G. Kasper (Eds.) *Cross-cultural Pragmatics: Requests and Apologies* (pp. 221–47). Norwood, NJ: Ablex.

Fearm-Banks, K. (2002). *Crisis Communication: A Casebook Approach*. New Jersey: Lawrence Erlbaum Associates Publishers.

Goodwin, C., & Ross, I. (1992). Consumer responses to service failures: Influence of procedural and interactional fairness perceptions. *Journal of Business Research*, 25, 149–163.

Graff, G., & Birkenstein, C. (2010). *They Say: The Moves that Matter in Academic Writing*. W.W. Norton & Company.

Hareli, S., & Weiner, B. (2002). Social emotions and personality inferences: A scaffold for a new direction in the study of achievement motivation. *Educational Psychologist*, 37, 183–193.

Hearit, K.M. (1995). 'Mistakes were made': Organizations, apologia, and crises of social legitimacy. *Communication Studies*, 46, 1–17.

Johnson, P.R., & Indvik, J. (2002). Integration theory: Development effective 'bad news' messages. *Business Communication Quarterly*, 55(3), 57–58.

Jung, Y. (2009). Korea. In F. Bargiela-Chiappini (Ed.) *The Handbook of Business Discourse* (pp. 356–371). Edinburgh: Edinburgh University Press.

Jung, Y. (2014). *Basics of Organizational Writing: A Critical Reading Approach*. Bern: Peter Lang.

Jung, Y. (2017). *Professional Writing: A Discourse Analysis Approach*. Singapore: Cengage Learning.

Kim, S. Avery, E., & Lariscy, R. (2009). Are crisis communicators practicing what we preach?: An evaluation of crisis response strategy analyzed in public relations research from 1991 to 2009. *Public Relations Review*, 35, 446–448.

Lee, B.K. (2004). Audience-oriented approach to crisis communication: A study of Hong Kong consumers' evaluation of an organizational crisis. *Communication Research*, 31, 600–618.

Lee, S., & Chung, S. (2012). Corporate apology and crisis communication: The effect of responsibility admittance and sympathetic expression on public's anger relief. *Public Relations Review*, 38(5), 932–934.

Limaye, M. (1997). Further conceptualization of explanation in negative messages. *Business Communication Quarterly*, 60(2), 38–50.

Locker, K., Mackiewicz, J., & Kienzler, D. (2018). *Business and Administrative Communication* (12th ed.). McGraw-Hill Education.

McDonald, L.M., Sparks, B., & Glendon, A.I. (2010). Stakeholder reactions to company crisis communication and causes. *Public Relations Review*, 36, 263–271.

Milkovich, G.T., & Newman, J.M. (2005). *Compensation* (8th ed.) New York: McGraw-Hill.

Moon, B.B., & Rhee, Y. (2012). Message strategies and forgiveness during crises: Effects of causal attributions and apology appeal types on forgiveness. *Journalism & Mass Communication Quarterly*, 89, 677–694.

Nadler, A., & Liviatan, I. (2006). Intergroup reconciliation: Effects of adversary's expressions of empathy, responsibility, and recipients' trust. *Personality and Social Psychology Bulletin*, 32, 459–470.

Pace, K.M., Fediuk, T.A., & Botero, I.C. (2010). The acceptance of responsibility and expressions of regret in organizational apologies after a transgression. *Corporate Communications: An International Journal*, 15, 410–427.

Patel, A., & Reinsch, L. (2003). Companies can apologize: Corporate apologies and legal liability. *Business Communication Quarterly*, 66, 9–25.

Ries, A., & Trout, J. (2000). *Positioning: The Battle for your Mind*. Boston, MA:McGraw-Hill.

7 Korean CEO's online greetings

7.1 Function of a CEO's online greetings

Media are the primary means by which organizations can reach targeted audiences and interact with key publics (Heath 1997). Media selection has become a strategic, unique challenge of specific business situations to support relationships with different types of internal and external partners (van den Hooff et al. 2005). Historically, business professionals prefer traditional media, including face-to-face communication, telephone, letters, and memos (George et al. 2013). Nevertheless, media preferences change over time due to technological innovations and associated changes in business communication practices (e.g., new media, such as electronic mail and voicemail) (Anders et al. 2020). Prospecting and relationship building may be uniquely facilitated by media that enable a responsive, audience-centric approach. Given the challenge of managing time and information in contemporary professional environments, the efficient and effective style of communication supported by the internet may help build prospect goodwill and support information-based interest in establishing new relationships. Technological innovation and changing communication practices directly affect the strategic rationales for choosing media, even for transmitting the greetings of the chief executive officer (CEO) to stakeholders. Organizations have multiple groups of people who have various 'stakes' and whose needs must be met in a variety of ways for the organization to thrive. Stakeholders include groups such as employees, stockholders, customers, suppliers, vendors, the media, and so forth. A CEO's greeting texts are chosen as major data of the chapter. It is because a CEO's online greeting might be the most fundamental genre to facilitate interaction with key stakeholders among many other public relations communication genres. A CEO's online greeting is posted on the company website for all to see so that all the stakeholders can easily access it. Nevertheless, presumably, it is likely to be seen by CEOs

DOI: 10.4324/9781003108061-7

as less important internally than externally, as major readership may be outside the company. This chapter aims to help stakeholders make sense of organizational behaviors and words which can be manipulated and shaped from corporate codes of conduct, guidelines for appropriate behavior in certain organizations. It explores how a Korean CEO's online greeting messages are crafted. Special attention is paid to which language codes are highlighted in the representative corporate voice genre. It tries to address the following research questions: How does PR communication realize in a CEO's online greetings? Which code of conduct is highlighted? What language features might a CEO consider to initiate and guide corporate activities? What are key textual components in the language of management? The complexity of management's concerns and its language choice to articulate the concerns are expected to tell us each company's exclusive keyword-based management language. This chapter illustrates textual features related to the corporate code of conduct (Jung 2012). It explicates companies' codes of conduct generally illustrated by corporate value, sustainability, and corporate social responsibility. Eccles and Nohria's (1992) strategic triadic is used as a primary framework for data analysis (unit for data analysis, exclusively). The strategic triadic is composed of three interdependent elements – action, identity, and rhetoric – and the three elements are the basis for effective management. *Action* refers to activities to fulfill organizational goals or revise performance expectations. Intertwined with action is 'how *identities* get built and maintained in organizations, and how the quest for personal identity . . . is an inseparable aspect of everything that occurs' (Eccles and Nohria 1992:12). Integral to action and identity is *rhetoric* or 'the way human beings interact to get things done' and 'how language is used to shape the way people think and act' (Eccles and Nohria 1992: 9–10). Rhetoric's tools include the choice of words (subjects, verbs, modifiers), structure, metaphors, and stories that define and influence. Strategic rhetoric, they contend, is purposeful, as in functioning corporate vision statements. In this section, language components as units for data analysis accommodate 'rhetoric as (nominalized) action'. That is, this section explores textual features related to action for fulfilling organizational goals involving nouns and noun phrases (e.g., *cisokcekin sengkwa*, 'sustainable achievement'; *sangsayng*, 'co-prosperity') and/or nominalized verbs (e.g., *kokaykuy chapyelhwatoyn kachi ceykong*, 'creating value for the customer'). Accordingly, language components in the section are seen as an agent to conduct business work in daily operations and an instrument to get business work done or to provide direction for the way things get done. After investigating some genre-specific features of a Korean CEO's online greetings, this chapter explores their language components.

7.2   A Korean CEO's online greeting as a volition-oriented genre

The volition/prediction modal *will* has two different types of meaning, which can be labeled intrinsic and extrinsic (Biber et al. 1999). Intrinsic modality refers to actions and events that humans (or other agents) directly control: meanings relating to volition (or intention). Extrinsic modality refers to the logical status of events or states, usually relating to prediction. There are two typical structural correlates of modal verbs with intrinsic meanings: (1) the subject of the verb phrase usually refers to a human being (as an agent of the main verb), and (2) the main verb is usually a dynamic verb, describing an activity or event that can be controlled. In contrast, modal verbs with extrinsic meanings usually occur with non-human subjects and/or with main verbs having stative meanings. In this respect, intrinsic modality is relevant to action, whereas extrinsic modality is regarding the state. The function of extrinsic modality goes along well with the claim that business writing is a sort of self-effacing. Namely, a state is of importance much more than an action with a human agent. 'What did [non-human agent] happen?' is emphasized much more than 'What did [human agent] do?' in business context (Jung 2017). This is due to the primary transactional (rather than interactional) function of official or formal business communication, such as conveying objective information. Contrary to this, a Korean CEO's online greetings are action-oriented with no subject or, to a lesser extent, with a non-human subject, such as the name of a corporation.

On the one hand, being a situation-oriented language, Korean allows all major constituents of sentences to be left unexpressed if discoursally or situationally recoverable. As Sohn (1999: 401) claims, in interpersonal encounters, the pronouns referring to the speaker and hearer are usually not expressed unless focused or delimited. The omission of subject pronouns in a Korean CEO's online greetings is also owing to the characteristic of business communication as agentless (see the omission of a sentential subject, *we*, in examples 24 and 25, among many other data in this chapter). Cheney (1991: 5) also notes that organizational messages take on a relatively placeless, nameless, omniscient quality, even when a corporate identity is assumed and declared.

On the other hand, the company's name representing a non-human subject may serve a similar function to business *we*. Corporate voice is that disembodied *we* often used in statements by those representing the organization. It is used when the organization makes a public announcement or participates in a social debate, as well as whose interests are being served as it does so (Meisenbach and McMillan 2006: 123). In this respect, the most common use of first person in business writing is plural (*we, us, our*), not singular (*I*, *me*, *my*). The function of *we* is far from that of school grammar (i.e., inclusive *we*). We, as used in business writing exclusively for external communication, is called the business *we*. According to Brown and Levinson (1987: 202), *we* is used to indicate "'I" + *powerful* which is a corporate identity' (emphasis given). That is, *we* serve the function of being an organization excluding the other party. Despite the high frequency of the use of non-human subjects or having no subjects in a Korean CEO's online greetings, the modal is used to mark volition showing a dynamic or active meaning, not states relating to prediction. This claim is exemplified by the following two samples of a Korean CEO's online greetings.

Example 24

Korean text	English translation
xx는 '최고의 제품과 서비스를 통한 사회공헌'이라는 경영이념을 실현하고자 노력을 기울여 왔습니다. xx는 최근 6년간 브랜드 상승률 세계 1위 기업이 되었습니다. 종합 전자업체로서의 글로벌 브랜드 구축이 고객 및 주주 여러분의 지속적인 관심과 애정이 바탕이 된 만큼, xx는 '고객과 주주를 최우선으로 하는 경영'을 펼쳐 나가기 위해 ①최선을 다할 것을 약속드리겠습니다. 초일류 기업으로 도약하기 위한 ②신성장 모멘텀을 확보하는데 주력하고, 디지털 시대에 맞는 ③초일류 조직문화를 창조해 나가겠습니다. 나눔과 상생의 경영을 실천하고, 보다 풍요로운 사회를 위해 기업의 사회적 책임을 다함으로써 ④지속적으로 성장해 나가기 위해 노력하겠습니다.	xx has made every effort to realize the management philosophy of 'Social Contribution through Best Products and Services'. xx has become the world's number one brand growth rate in the past six years. Building a global brand as a comprehensive electronics company has been based on the continued interest and affection of customers and shareholders. ①xx <u>promises to do its best</u> to pursue management that puts customers and shareholders first. ②<u>(We) will focus on securing new growth momentum</u> to become a top-notch company and ③<u>create a top-notch organizational culture</u> suitable for the digital age. ④<u>(We) will strive to grow continuously</u> by practicing sharing and win-win management and fulfilling corporate social responsibilities for a more prosperous society.

Example 25

Korean text	English translation
xx는 고객의 차별화된 가치를 제공하는 것이 사업의 목적입니다. 고객의 숨은 요구를 찾아내고 고객 만족을 실현할 수 있는 제품과 서비스를	xx aims to provide differentiated value for customers. ①<u>(We) will lead the market</u> by establishing a system that can respond to market trends by discovering the hidden needs of

(*Continued*)

Korean text	English translation
출시함으로써 시장 트랜드에 대응할 수 있는 체제를 갖추어 ①시장을 선도해 나가겠습니다. 미래의 변화를 주도하기 위해 미래 역량에 대한 투자를 확대해 나감으로써 ②필요한 역량확보에 만전을 기하겠습니다. ③xx의 미래를 담보할 새로운 성장동력을 발굴하고 육성해 나가겠습니다. 가치 창출의 원천인 ④우수 인재 확보를 위한 노력을 강화하겠습니다. 시장과 고객가치 중심으로 일의 우선순위를 재편하여 지속적인 성과를 창출할 수 있는 ⑤강한 조직을 만들어 나가겠습니다. 구성원들의 창의성이 최대한 발휘될 수 있는 ⑥조직 문화 조성에 만전을 기하겠습니다. 주주 가치를 최우선으로 하는 경영을 통해 xx 를 ⑦일등 기업으로 발전시켜 나갈 것을 약속하겠습니다.	customers and launching products and services that can realize customer satisfaction. In order to lead the change in the future, ②(We) will make every effort to secure necessary capabilities by expanding investment in future capabilities. ③(We) will discover and nurture new growth engines to secure xx's future. ④(We) will strengthen our efforts to secure talented people who are the source of value creation. ⑤(We) will create a strong organization that can create sustainable performance by recognizing our work priorities based on market and customer values. ⑥(We) will make every effort to create an organizational culture where members' creativity can be maximized. ⑦(We) promise to develop xx into a leading company through management that puts shareholder value first.

The modal is not with progressive aspect, marking future events or situations that will take place over a period of time in both examples above. Modality in the above Korean CEO's online greetings serves the function of volition or intention in that the Korean modal suffix -*keyss* (겠) denotes the speaker's attitude on modality toward the content of the sentence (①, ②, ③, and ④, in example 24; ①, ②, ③, ④, ⑤, ⑥, and ⑦, in example 25). The simple future is commonly used to mark public volition involving public agency (rather than personal volition involving personal agency) there. The simple aspect *will* in this context would suggest a strong volitional meaning. This pattern occurs a high proportion of the time, with the volitional aspect following no subject or non-human subjects in a Korean CEO's online greetings.

7.3   Organizational credibility in a CEO's online greetings

Keyword-based management language in a CEO's online greetings can address how issues are framed for readers. *Genre theory provides a foundation for examining a CEO's online greeting paragraph structure.* Seminal genre analysts' work (i.e., Swales 1990; Bhatia 1993) has a tendency to explicate language use through formal and functional aspects of discourse (e.g., move structure and intertextuality) in a *conventionalized* communicative setting. Swales (1990, 2002) defines genre based on communicative purposes. He describes genre as a class of communicative events characterized by a set of communicative purposes. According to him, communicative purposes are highlighted as a fundamental feature that sets constraints for the stylistic and linguistic choices of the genre. Communicative purposes as a fundamental feature in defining genres are relevant to the first step when planning communication (e.g., 'Is the writer's message mainly to deliver objective information?' 'Is it mainly persuasive?' 'Or is it to create solidarity?'). All messages have an underlying purpose. For example, the purpose of a credit refusal letter is to refuse the request while encouraging the customer's continued business. Creating goodwill is especially important when communicating unwelcome news with business partners. According to major genre analysts (Swales 1990; Bhatia 1993), the arrangement of text constitutes the rhetorical moves. Swales (1990) introduces rhetorical moves as an essential part of the valid rhetorical structure for socio-cognitive genre analysis because they remarkably orient to the task and purpose of the text. Moves are functional units of texts and describe their communicative purposes. Therefore, moves can be basic elements of a certain genre. For example, Swales (1981) assigns a typical four-move structure to the introduction of research articles using the data from 48 article introductions, such as establishing the research field, summarizing previous research, preparing for the present research, and introducing the present research. The order in which the writer presents his or her ideas is as important as the ideas themselves realized as atomic paragraphs. This section classifies the atomic paragraphs establishing credentials into two corporate values and some elements of corporate social legitimacy. On the one hand, particular codes of conduct as each organization's value for establishing credentials are highlighted with the two value strategies, such as differentiation and association. On the other hand, two elements of corporate social legitimacy are explored, competence and community, with the labels of sustainability and corporate social responsibility, respectively.

7.3.1 *Corporate values*

Cheney and Christensen (2001: 232) argue that many organizations have begun to realize the difficulties of convincing an external audience about their deeds if the internal audience does not accept the message – and vice versa. Organizational communicators must be certain to create consistent messages that are persuasive to both groups. Organizations enter situations with a preexisting reputation that may make persuasion or promotion easier (e.g., marketing). Audiences may have developed beliefs and attitudes about the reputation of a particular organization that can make it easier for the speaker to persuade the audience. The complex nature of organizational credibility is explained in part by calculus-based trust, trust based on the ongoing calculability of others' behavior (e.g., identity, values, beliefs, and goals) (Crichton 2013). This claim is exemplified by the use of some eclectic management languages (e.g., *cungcangki picenin kokaykul uyhan hyeksin*, 'innovation for customers as a mid-to-long-term vision'; *kokaykul choywusenulo hanun kyengyengchelhak*, 'business philosophy placing customers as the highest priority').

Corporate value is the central, enduring character projected by an organization, and it illustrates that organizational identity refers to those core, distinctive, and enduring features unique to an institution (Kuhn 1997; Aust 2004). It is concerned with how audiences perceive the organization, not just with how the organization sees or presents itself. Organizational value is sometimes understood as how the organization wishes to be seen and sometimes as how the organization is actually perceived by audiences. In this respect, its messages attempt to persuade audience members about who an organization is, what it does, and what it stands for. By central character of the organization, the corporate communicators mean those practices, values, and so forth that are at the core of who the organization is. This may include the products the organization produces or sells, the services that it provides, its status as a family-owned company, or its affiliation with a larger organization.

Values are generally agreed-upon ideas of what is right or wrong or good and bad in a society. Schuetz (1990) argues that organizations tell their stories through value claims that make judgments about people, actions, objects, and ideas. Zorn et al. (2000) highlight the importance of advocating organizational values. They argue that the values of service, quality, and excellence are pervasive in contemporary organizational rhetoric on change. Bostdorff and Vibbert (1994) have paid particular attention to how values are used in organizational communication. After studying many organizational messages, they concluded that organizations use a practice called values advocacy in much of their rhetoric. They advocate the claim that values accomplish one of three goals. First, appeals to values may be used to enhance the image of the organization. By referencing things that are viewed by the audience as good or right, organizational communicators can create positive overall thoughts about the organization. Second, appeals to values may be able to help minimize the impact of criticism or an organization. Finally, appeals to values may be used to help prepare audiences to accept future arguments about policy issues. As a piece of empirical research work on linguistic realization on corporate values, Jung (2012) deals with nature of public relations communication articulated in the different codes of conduct published by three Korean companies. He exemplifies that each company differentiates online public relations communication. He suggests linguistic code of conduct that Korean CEOs highlight when formulating online messages for stakeholders. He investigates whether the code is properly incorporated into a CEO's online public relations communication and whether companies put stress on different codes of conduct incorporated into corporate value, corporate philosophy, business and/or management principle, and corporate vision. His study illustrates that unlike each corporation's official key values, highlighted values in CEO's online greetings show their actual 'orientation to work' (Watson 2008). In other words, 'the degree of intensity' is differentiated by CEOs in the choice of management's language (Ran and Duimering 2007). Jung's (2012) claim that CEO's particular language choices might be in an 'attempt to purposefully communicate the values of the organization and the preferences of leaders' (Hartelius and Browning 2008: 18). Given the claim, this section is going to explore what type of management language is stressed and valued in a Korean CEO's online greetings. It illustrates that a particular code of conduct as a key corporate value is highlighted across companies with the two value strategies, *differentiation* and *association* (Bostdorff and Vibbert 1994).

7.3.1.1   Differentiation

Since one of the goals of value-creation rhetoric is to create a distinct impression of the organization, some messages need to demonstrate what is unique about the organization. The organization must show how its services are unique. No matter which specific appeal is used, the overall goal is to distinguish or differentiate the organization from similar organizations competing for customers. Organizations differentiate themselves from the competition. The idea of claimed distinctiveness is fairly self-explanatory. An organization's value is composed in part by what makes it different from other similar organizations. Their distinctiveness is likely to be made from their competitors if they wish to have clear, strong values. A distinct and attractive value may encourage audience members to identify with an organization. For instance, the value of *kullopel cwungsim* ('global orientation') in the following example is highest in frequency (e.g., ①*kullopel kyengyengcheycey kwuchwuk* [글로벌 경영체계 구축], 'establishing a global management system'; ②*kullopel catongcha meyikhe* [글로벌 자동차 메이커], 'global car maker'; ③*kullopel ritelo toyak* [글로벌 리더로 도약],

'taking the leap to becoming a global leader'; ④*kullopel sayngsankecemuy kyengyeng ancenghwa* [글로벌 생산거점의 경영 안정화], 'management stabilization of global manufacturing footprints'; ⑤*kullopel choillyu kiepulo sengcang* (글로벌 초일류 기업으로 성장), 'developing into a global no. 1 corporation'; ⑥*kullopel sahoykonghen hwaltong* (글로벌 사회공헌 활동), 'taking global corporate social responsibility'; ⑦*cisokkanunghan phungyorowun miraylul yelekanun kullopel kiep* (지속가능한 풍요로운 미래를 열어가는 글로벌기업), 'a global company that opens a sustainable and prosperous future').

Example 26

Korean text	English translation
xx는 중장기 비전인 '고객을 위한 혁신'_을 목표로 지속적인 ①글로벌 경영체제 구축과 품질향상을 통해 브랜드 가치가 상승하고 있습니다.	With the aim of 'Innovation for Customers', which is a mid-to-long-term vision, xx's brand value is rising through a continuous ①global management system and quality improvement.
xx는 ②글로벌자동차메이커 로자리매김하고있습니다. xx는 ③글로벌리더로도약해나갈것 입니다. 미국, 중국, 인도, 유럽등 ④글로벌생산거점의경영안정화 를통해 ⑤글로벌초일류기업으로 성장할수있는기반을갖추었습니다. 고객을최우선으로하는 경영철학을반영하여브랜드와 감성품질수준을향상시켜 xx의가치를더욱높이겠습니다.	xx has established itself as ②a global automaker. xx will continue ③to leap forward as a global leader. (We) have established the foundation ⑤to grow into a leading global company by ④stabilizing the management of global production bases in the United States, China, India, and Europe. We will enhance the value of xx by improving the brand and emotional quality level by reflecting a management philosophy that puts customers first.
동반성장을위한상생경영을강화하고 ⑥글로벌사회공헌활동을확대하여성 숙한기업시민으로서의책임을다하겠 습니다. 지구촌인류행복의근원인환 경을위한기술을개발보급하여 ⑦지속가능한풍요로운미래를열 어가는글로벌기업 이되겠습니다.	(We) will fulfill our responsibilities as mature corporate citizens by strengthening win-win management for mutual growth and ⑥expanding global social contribution activities. (We) will become ⑦a global company that opens a sustainable and prosperous future by developing and distributing technologies for the environment, the source of human happiness in the global village.

Unlike example 26, *excellence* is the most highly valued in example 27 (①1 *uy* [1위], '1st'; ②*seykyeychoycho* [세계최초], 'world's first'; ③*cho* [초], 'first'; ④*cho* [초], 'first'; and ⑤*cho* [초], 'first').

Example 27

Korean text	English translation
고객 여러분의 한결같은 사랑 덕분에 xx은 국내 3대 고객 만족도 조사에서 최장 기간 연속 ①1위를 지켜오며 대한민국 대표 ICT 회사로 인정받을 수 있었습니다.	Thanks to the unwavering love of our customers, xx was able to be recognized as Korea's representative ICT company by maintaining ①the top spot for the longest period of time in Korea's top three customer satisfaction surveys.
xx은 ②세계 최초 5G 상용화라는 통신의 진화를 이끈 힘을 바탕으로 기존 한계를 뛰어넘는 '③초(超)혁신'을 통해 고객 여러분의 삶의 질을 높이고 대한민국 산업이 발전할 수 있는 변화의 촉매제가 되고자 합니다.	Based on the power that led the evolution of telecommunications, ②the world's first commercialization of 5G, xx aims to improve the quality of life of customers through '③super innovation' that goes beyond the existing limits and become a catalyst for change that can advance the Korean industry.
인공지능(AI)과 Data경쟁력을 활용하여 AI·Mobility 영역에서 고객 여러분의 기대를 뛰어넘는 '④초(超)생활' 서비스를 출시하고, 미래 산업 혁신 방향을 제시하며 '⑤초(超)산업' 시대를 열겠습니다.	Utilizing artificial intelligence (AI) and data competitiveness, we launched a '④super life' service that exceeds customers' expectations in the field of AI and mobility and suggests the direction of future industry innovation. (We) will usher in an era of '⑤super-industry'.

7.3.1.2   *Association*

The strategy of association is the opposite of the strategy of differentiation. One way in which organizations build values is by associating or connecting themselves with things that are viewed positively by their audience. The rhetorical strategy of values advocacy is key to the strategy of association. Value appeals in organizational rhetoric are often statements meant to demonstrate that the values of the organization align with the values of the audience or society in general (Hoffman and Ford 2010). When using the common ground technique, organizations demonstrate that they share things in common with the audience. Individuals are more likely to identify with an organization that aligns itself with goals, values, and ideas similar to their own. Organizations can use identification strategies to emphasize the core elements of the organization that will not be altered (e.g., *co-prosperity*, as in *sangsaynguy kyengyengul silchen*, 'fulfilling co-prosperity management'). The strategy of association is relevant to empathy talk, defined as listening attentively to assess the addressee's need for empathy and providing him or her with the necessary communicative responses to meet that need expeditiously (Clark et al. 2013). It may accomplish its promotional goals in part by using empathy to make audience members more receptive to the ideas being presented (e.g., showing willingness to make customers happy). An ethical code, *hayngpok* (행복, 'happiness'), is articulated in example 28 (①*wulilul hayngpokhakey haycwunun ket* [우리를 행복하게 해주는 것], 'what makes us happy'; ②*cakun saynghwaluy hayngpok* [작은 생활의 행복], 'happiness in small life'; ③*kacang khun hayngpokul cwunun kiep* [가장 큰 행복을 주는 기업], 'the company that gives you the greatest happiness'; ④*hayngpokul cwunun chinkwu* [행복을 주는 친구], 'friend who brings happiness'; ⑤*kokayknimuy te khun hayngpokul wuyhay noleyk* [고객님의 더 큰 행복을 위해 노력], 'our best for the greater happiness of our customers').

Example 28

Korean text	English translation
세상이 아무리 변해도 ①우리를행복하게해주는것은 ②작은생활의행복이라고 생각합니다. xx가 원하는 것은 이런 것입니다. 가장 많이 파는 기업보다, ③가장큰행복 을주는기업이고 싶습니다.	No matter has much the world changes, (we) believe ①what makes us happy is ②the happiness of a small life. This is what xx wants. (We) want to be ③the company that gives the greatest happiness rather than the company that sells the most.
언제나 고객님의 곁에서 ④행복을주는친구가 되었다고 자부합니다. 앞으로도 맛있는 밥과 더불어 건강한 물, 청결한 위생으로 고객님의 건강한 생활을 책임지는 좋은 친구가 되겠습니다.	(We) pride ourselves on being ④ a friend who always brings happiness to our customers. (We) will continue to be a good friend who takes responsibility for the healthy life of our customers through healthy water and clean hygiene along with delicious rice.
국내를 넘어 세계인의 마음을 사로잡아 한국을 대표하는 기업이 되는 모습, 함께 지켜봐 주시고 응원해주십시오. ⑤고객님의더큰행복을위해 노력하겠습니다.	Please watch and support us as we become a company that represents Korea by capturing the hearts of people not only in Korea but also around the world. (We) will do ⑤our best for the greater happiness of our customers.

In a similar vein, the association links to *you*-attitude. *You*-attitude considers how the message is recognized and perceived by the audience, as opposed to the actual content of the message realized by the speaker or the writer. As an emphatic device for highlighting the reader's primary interest, *you* can play a role in illustrating that the writer values the reader. *Kokayk* (고객, 'customer') replacing *you* is often used in the following examples in order to highlight that the writer orients to the reader. In the following examples, *kokayk cwungsim* (고객중심) 'customer focus' is most intensified (e.g. ①*kokayk cwungsimul choywusen kachi* (고객중심을 최우선 가치) 'put customers first' ②*kokayki wonhanun ketul kacang ppaluko yuyenhakey ceykonghanun kiep* (고객이 원하는 것을 가장 빠르고 유연하게 제공하는 기업) 'The fastest and most flexible company that provides what customers want', ③*kokayk han salam han salamul sayngkakhanun maum* (고객 한 사람 한 사람을 생각하는 마음) 'A heart that cares for each customer' in example 29; ①*ku cwungsimeynun enceyna kokayk* (그 중심에는 언제나 고객) 'The customer been at the center of it', ②*kokaykkuy salmul tewuk kachi isskey mantulki uyhay kkunhimepsi nolyek* (고객의 삶을 더욱 가치있게 만들기 위해 끊임없이 노력) 'constant effort to make the lives of our customers more valuable', ③*kokaykkuy ilsangul pakkwunun saylowun tocen* (고객의 일상을 바꾸는 새로운 도전) 'a new challenge that changes the daily life of customers', ④*kokaykkuy ilsangul ciwen* (고객의 일상을 지원) 'supporting customers' daily life', ⑤*kokayk yelepwunuy sengweney pantusi pwuung* (고객 여러분의 성원에 반드시 부응) 'Be sure to respond to the support of our customers' in example 30; ①*kokayknimi kyeysyesskiey onuluy xx unhayngi concay* (고객님이 계셨기에 오늘의 xx 은행이 존재) 'Today's xx bank exists because of your presence', ②*kokaykkuy khusin salangkwa cinsimul saykye kokayknimkkey te khun mitumkwa sinloylo potap* (고객의 크신 사랑과 진심을 새겨, 고객님께 더 큰 믿음과 신뢰로 보답하는 xx은행) 'Engraving the customer's great love and sincerity, repaying customers with greater belief and trust', ③*kokayknim motwuuy kacengey kenkangkwa hayngpoki katukhasikil kiwen* (고객님 모두의 가정에 건강과 행복이 가득하시길 기원) 'Wishing you and your family health and happiness' in example 31).

Example 29

Korean text	English translation
xx는 지난 100여년간 대한민국 ICT를 이끌어온 통신종가로서 ①고객중심을최우선가치로 두고 혁신적인 기술과 서비스를 주도하는 기업이 되겠습니다. ②고객이원하는것을가장빠르고 유연하게제공하는기업, 다양한 산업의 혁신을 리딩하는 기업으로서 대한민국의 발전을 위해 최선을 다하겠습니다. ③고객 한사람한사람을 생각하는마음을 담아 따뜻한 기술로 더 나은 미래를 만들어 가기 위해 노력하는 xx의 모습을 지켜봐 주시기 바랍니다.	As a telecommunication leader that has led Korea's ICT for the past 100 years, xx will become a company that leads innovative technologies and services with ①customer-centricity as the top priority. (We) will do our best for the development of Korea as ②a company that provides customers with the fastest and most flexibly what they want, a company that leads innovation in various industries. Please keep an eye on xx's effort to create a better future with warm technology with ③a heart that cares for each and every customer.

Example 30

Korean text	English translation
xx는 남보다 한 발 앞서 생각하고 움직임으로써 업계에 새로운 바람을 불러 일으켜 왔습니다. 그리고 ①그중심엔언제나고객이 있었습니다. ②고객의삶을더욱가치있게만들기 위해끊임없이노력해 왔습니다.	xx has created a new wind in the industry by thinking and moving one step ahead of others. And ①<u>the customer has always been at the center</u> of it. (We) have been ②<u>constantly</u> <u>striving to make the lives of our</u> <u>customers more valuable.</u>
이제 xx는 5G 시대를 맞아 ③고객의일상을바꾸는새로운도전을 하고 있습니다. 보다 행복하고 즐거우며 감동이 있는 ④고객의일상을지원하기 위해 xx는 남이 아직 가보지 못한 길을 가려 합니다.	Now, in the 5G era, xx is taking on ③<u>a new challenge that will change</u> <u>the daily life of its customers.</u> In order ④ <u>to support the daily life of our</u> <u>customers</u> who are happier, and more impressed. xx is going down a path that others have not yet taken.
앞으로도 xx가 만드는 변화와 혁신을 애정 어린 관심으로 지켜봐 주십시오. ⑤고객여러분의성원에 반드시부응할 수 있도록 전 임직원이 열정과 헌신을 아끼지 않겠습니다.	Please continue to watch the changes and innovations that xx makes with affectionate interest in the future. All executives and employees will spare no effort in their passion and dedication so that we can ⑤<u>meet the support of our</u> <u>customers.</u>

Example 31

Korean text	English translation
지난 100년간 숱한 시련과 위기도 있었지만, 사시사철 늘 푸른 솔과 같이 xx은행을 한결같이 믿고 응원해주신 ①고객님이 계셨기에 오늘의 xx은행이 존재한다고 생각합니다. 앞으로도 ②고객의 크신 사랑과 진심을 새겨, 고객님께 더 큰 믿음과 신뢰로 보답하는 xx은행이 되겠습니다.	There have been many trials and crises over the past 100 years, but (we) believe that ①<u>today's XX Bank exists because</u> <u>there were customers</u> who always believed in and supported XX Bank like a blue pine tree all year round. In the future, (we) will continue to be ②<u>XX Bank that</u> <u>repays customers with greater trust and</u> <u>trust by engraving the great love and</u> <u>sincerity of our customers.</u>
xx은행에 대한 변함없는 관심과 성원을 부탁드리며, ③고객님모두의가정에건강과행복 이가득하시길기원합니다.	(We) ask for your unwavering interest and support for XX Bank and ③<u>hope that all</u> <u>of our customers' families will be filled</u> <u>with health and happiness.</u>

7.3.2 Elements of corporate social legitimacy

Organizational credibility is explained in part by the theory of corporate social legitimacy (Hearit 1995). Although Hearit (1995) discusses corporate social legitimacy specifically in reference to rhetoric during a crisis, the concept seems useful for understanding how organizations can secure and maintain the social capital to operate in noncrisis situations as well. The contemporary notion of corporate social legitimacy helps tailor the traditional elements of credibility to the complex and unique idea of what it means for an organization to have credibility. Hearit explains that organizations are accepted only if they demonstrate a balance between the costs and benefits to the communities in which they operate. This balance is labeled corporate social legitimacy. Corporate social legitimacy is accomplished when an organization persuades the community that it possesses two characteristics: competence and community. The first element of corporate social legitimacy is *competence*. An organization must demonstrate that it can accomplish its goals – that it can produce a product or deliver a service that meets societal standards. An organization may find appeals to competence by identifying statements that claim that an organization's products or services are safe and effective or that vouch for the financial stability of the company.

The second element of corporate social legitimacy is *community*. An organization must demonstrate that it operates as a responsible member of the larger community. Hearit (1995: 3) explains that a corporation's actions must be ethically defensible; that is, its acts must demonstrate responsibility, create trust, and be legal. The following sections explore two elements, sustainability and corporate social responsibility, to establish corporate credibility.

7.3.2.1 Sustainability

An organization must demonstrate that it can accomplish its goals (i.e., producing a product or delivering a service that meets societal standards). This claim might link to the value of research and development (R&D), the heart of a company's activity that is concerned with applying the results of scientific research to create or develop new products and improve and/ or update existing ones in highlighting corporate sustainability. Example 32 exemplifies sustainability with the company's achievements in order to make the corporate competence objective and concrete (①*kwukkakikan-sanepkenseley cwutocekin yekhalul swuhayng* [국가기간산업건설에 주도적인 역할을 수행], 'playing a leading role in the construction of key national industries'; ②*swucheli saeppwunyaeyseto ttuyenan kiswullyekul pathangulo sicangul sentohanun kiepulo calimaykim* [수처리 사업분야에 서도 뛰어난 기술력을 바탕으로 시장을 선도하는 기업으로 자리매

김], 'to establish itself as a market-leading company based on outstanding technology in the water treatment business field'; ③*milayuy sinsengcang-tonglyekey tayhan cisokcekin yenkwukaypalkwa thwucalul hwaktay* [미래의 신성장동력에 대한 지속적인 연구개발과 투자를 확대], 'to expand R&D and investment in new future growth engines').

Example 32

Korean text	English translation
저희 xx은 xx년 창립 이후 50년이 넘는 기간동안 대한민국의 건설역사에 큰 획을 그어온 국내의 대표적인 건설사로써, 이 기간 동안 ①<u>국가기간산업건설에주도적인역할을수행</u>해 왔습니다. 아울러, 최고의 주거 브랜드인 xx과 xx를 성공적으로 런칭하고, 베트남과 두바이 등 해외건설시장에 적극적으로 진출하여 선진기업문화 전도사로서의 역할도 충실히 수행하고 있습니다. 특히 xx 및 xx 공사에서는 타의 추종을 불허하는 기술력으로 xx, xx 공사를 성공적으로 준공하며 해외시장 관계자들의 극찬을 이끌어내기도 했습니다.	We, xx company, have been ①<u>playing a leading role in the construction of key national industries</u> as a representative construction company in Korea that has made a big mark in the construction history of Korea for more than 50 years since its foundation in xx. In addition, (we) have successfully launched xx and xx, the best residential brands and actively entered overseas construction markets, such as Vietnam and Dubai, fulfilling our role as an evangelist of an advanced corporate culture. In particular, in xx and xx construction, (we) successfully completed xx and xx construction with unmatched technological prowess, drawing praise from stakeholders in the overseas market.
또한, 저희 xx은 미래의 블루오션으로 떠오른 ②<u>수처리사업분야에서도뛰어난 기술력을바탕으로시장을선도하는 기업으로자리매김</u> 했습니다. 발전 · 플랜트 · 물산업 등 ③<u>미래의 신성장동력에대한지속적인연구개발과투자를확대</u>하겠습니다.	In addition, we, xx, have ②<u>established itself as a market-leading company based on outstanding technology in the water treatment business field</u>, which has emerged as a blue ocean of the future. (We) will continue ③<u>to expand R&D and investment in new future growth engines</u>, such as power plants, plants, and water industries.

Unlike example 32, which makes a concrete explanation of establishing sustainability, example 33 seems relatively abstract in emphasizing the company's sustainability. It is because the following company's management strategy calls for solely *kkwucwunhan sengcang* (꾸준한 성장, 'steady growth') as a token of the company's sustainability, as shown in ①*cal pethimyense chaksilhi sengcang* (잘 버티면서 착실히 성장), 'hold up well and steady growth'; ②*kkwucwunhan celyek* (꾸준한 저력), 'steady power'; ③*kkwutkkwuthan caseywa ttwuksim* (꿋꿋한 자세와 뚝심), 'steadfast attitude and perseverrance'; ④*cisokkanung kiep* (지속가능 기업), 'sustainable company'; and ⑤*kkwutkkwuthakey* (꿋꿋하게), 'steadfast'.

Example 33

Korean text	English translation
현대 사회에서 기업의 경영환경은 실로 변화무쌍합니다. 좋을 때도 있지만 좋지 않을 때가 더 많습니다. 물론 좋지 않은 환경에서 ①잘 버티면서 착실히 성장해 나가는 것이 누구나 기대하는 좋은 기업의 스텐더드 모델입니다. 급격한 외부환경 변화에 적응하는 것도 쉽지 않은 일이지만, 더 큰 어려움은 그 변화의 속도가 더욱 빨라지고 있다는 점입니다. 변화의 속도에 맞춰 일일이 신속한 대응을 하면 좋겠지만, 쉽지는 않아 보입니다. 그래서 ②꾸준한 저력을 갖추는 일이 더 소중합니다. ③웬만한 변화에도 흔들리지 않는 꿋꿋한 자세와 뚝심이 ④지속가능 기업의 핵심적 요소입니다. 앞으로도 ⑤외부 환경에 흔들리지 않고 꿋꿋하게 제 갈 길을 가겠습니다	In today's society, the business environment of companies is very changeable. Sometimes it's good, but more often than not, it's bad. Of course, it is ①the standard model of a good company that everyone expects to grow steadily while surviving in an unfavorable environment. It is not easy to adapt to rapid changes in the external environment, but the greater difficulty is that the pace of change is accelerating. It would be nice to respond quickly, one by one, in line with the speed of change, but it doesn't seem easy. That is why it is ②more important to have a steady potential. ③A steadfast attitude and perseverance that is not shaken by any change are ④the key elements of a sustainable company. (We) will ⑤continue to go our own way without being shaken by the external environment.

7.3.2.2 *Corporate social responsibility*

An organization must demonstrate that it operates as a responsible member of the larger community. Its acts must demonstrate responsibility, create trust, and be legal (Hearit 1995). Investigating the community and supporting local organizations can set a business brand apart from the rest. The organization might identify appeals designed to create community by looking for claims about the charitable activities of the organization or arguments that show that community members trust the organization. This claim is closely related to the concept of corporate social responsibility (CSR). Responsible business practices can improve public perception of a company's brand, as in the following example: *sahoycek chaykimul tahanun kiepulose ku concaykachilul tewuk pitnakey hakeyssum* (사회적 책임을 다하는 기업으로서 그 존재가치를 더욱 빛나게 하겠슴), 'to make its existence shine even more as a company that fulfills its social responsibilities'.

Example 34

Korean text	English translation
저희 회사는 '안정적인 수익기반을 갖춘 건실한 회사'로 거듭나기 위해 전 임직원이 하나가 되어 힘과 역량을 집중하고자 합니다. 아울러 단순히 성장과 이윤만을 추구하는 회사가 아닌, '아름다운 기업 DNA'를 주변 이웃과 지역사회에 널리 전파하며 <u>사회적 책임을 다하는 기업으로서 그 존재가치를 더욱 빛나게 하겠습니다.</u>	In order to be reborn as a 'sound company with a stable profit base', all executives and employees will unite and concentrate their strength and capabilities. In addition, we will not only pursue growth and profits but also spread the 'beautiful corporate DNA' to our neighbors and local communities, and (we) will <u>make its existence shine even more as a company that fulfills its social responsibilities.</u>

References

Anders, A.D., Coleman, J.T., & Castleberry, S.B. (2020). Communication preferences of business-to-business buyers for receiving initial sales messages: A comparison of media channels selection theories. *International Journal of Business Communication*, 57(3), 370–400.

Aust, P.J. (2004). Communicated values as indicators of organizational identity: A method for organizational assessment and its application in a case study. *Communication Studies*, 55, 515–534.

Bhatia, V. (1993). *Analysing Genre: Language Use in Professional Settings*. London: Longman.

Biber, D. Johansson, S., Leech, G., Conrad, S., & Finegan, E. (1999). *Longman Grammar of Spoken and Written English*. Harlow: Pearson Education.

Bostdorff, D.M., & Vibbert, S.L. (1994). Values advocacy: Enhancing organizational images, deflecting public criticism, and grounding future arguments. *Public Relations Review*, 20, 141–158.

Brown, P., & Levinson, S. (1987). *Politeness: Some Universals in Language Use*. Cambridge: Cambridge University Press.

Cheney, G. (1991). *Rhetoric in an Organizational Society: Managing Multiple Identities*. Columbia: University of South Carolina Press.

Cheney, G., & Christensen, L.T. (2001). Public relations as contested terrain: A critical response. In R. Heath (Ed.) *Handbook of Public Relations* (pp. 167–182). Thousand Oaks, CA: Sage.

Clark, C.M., Murfett, U.M., Rogers, P.S., & Ang, S. (2013). Is empathy effective for customer service? Evidence from call center interactions. *Journal of Business and Technical Communication*, 27(2), 123–153.

Crichton, J. (2013). 'Will there be flowers shoved at me?' A study in organizational trust, moral order and professional integrity. In C. Candlin & J. Crichton (Eds.) *Discourse of Trust* (pp. 119–132). Basingstoke: Palgrave Macmillan.

Eccles, R.G., & Nohria, N. (1992). *Beyond the Hype: Rediscovering the Essence of Management.* Cambridge, MA: Harvard Business School Press.

George, J.F., Carlson, J.R., & Valacich, J.S. (2013). Media selection as a strategic component of communication. *MIS Quarterly*, 37, 1233–1251.

Hartelius, E.J., & Browning, L.D. (2008). The application of rhetorical theory in managerial research: A literature review. *Management Communication Quarterly*, 22, 13–39.

Hearit, K.M. (1995). 'Mistakes were made': Organizations, apologia, and crises of social legitimacy. *Communication Studies*, 46, 1–17.

Heath, R.L. (1997). *Strategic Issues Management: Organizations and Public Policy Challenges.* Thousand Oaks, CA: Sage.

Hoffman, M., & Ford, P. (2010). *Organizational Rhetoric.* Thousand Oaks: Sage publications.

Jung, Y. (2012, April). Work orientation in Korean CEO's on-line greetings. *Online Journal of Communication and Media Technologies*, 2(2), 153–181.

Jung, Y. (2017). *Professional Writing: A Discourse Analysis Approach.* Singapore: Cengage Learning.

Kuhn, T. (1997). The discourse of issues management: A genre of organizational communication. *Communication Quarterly*, 45, 188–210.

Meisenbach, R.J., & McMillan, J. (2006). Blurring the boundaries: Historical dvelopments and future directions in organizational rhetoric. In C.S. Beck (Ed.) *Communication Yearbook 30* (pp. 99–141). Mahwah, NJ: Lawrence Erlbaum.

Ran, B., & Duimering, P.R. (2007). Imaging the organization: Language use in organizational identity claims. *Journal of Business and Technology Communication*, 21, 155–187.

Schuetz, J. (1990). Corporate advocacy as argumentation. In R.S. Trapp & J. Schuetz (Eds.) *Perspectives on Argumentation* (pp. 272–284). Prospect Heights, IL: Waveland Press.

Sohn, H-M. (1999). *The Korean Language.* Cambridge: Cambridge University Press.

Swales, J.M. (1981). Aspects of article introductions. *Asian ESP Research Report #1.* University of Aston, Birmingham.

Swales, J.M. (1990). *Genre Analysis: English in Academic and Research Settings.* Cambridge: Cambridge University Press.

Swales, J.M. (2002). On models of applied discourse analysis. In C. Candlin (Ed.) *Research and Practice in Professional Discourse* (pp. 61–77). Hong Kong: City University of Hong Kong Press.

van den Hooff, B., Groot, J., & de Jonge, S. (2005). Situational influences on the use of communication technologies: A meta-analysis and exploratory study. *Journal of Business Communication*, 42(4), 4–27.

Watson, T.J. (2008). Managing identity: Identity work, personal predicaments and structural circumstances. *Organization*, 15(1), 121–143.

Zorn, T.E., Page, D.J., & Cheney, G. (2000). Nuts about change: Multiple perspectives on change-oriented communication in a public sector organization. *Management Communication Quarterly*, 13, 515–566.

8   Concluding remarks

The world is becoming rapidly diverse, and people around the world are different. Cross-cultural communication involves a comparison between or among different cultures. Cross-cultural communicators analyze their own cultural values and practices, and then compare their differences. Cultural mistakes may damage the relational and/or transactional goals of international businesses. Cross-cultural differences need to be understood to prevent mistakes in communication across cultures. Cross-cultural communication knowledge is rather conventional (e.g., Hofstede's four cultural dimensions: individualism vs. collectivism, power distance, uncertainty avoidance vs. uncertainty tolerance, and masculinity vs. femininity). When clearly differentiated, cross-cultural communication knowledge can be useful for intercultural communication success. However, there is also the possibility that knowledge of cross-cultural communication may actually *cause* miscommunication in intercultural communication encounters, as illustrated in Chapter 4. Relatively speaking, intercultural communication knowledge is nonconventional or context-oriented in that intercultural communication occurs when people from different cultures communicate. Intercultural communication focuses on the moment when communication across cultures is taking place. In this respect, it is more advanced than a cross-cultural communication approach involving the acquisition of atomistic information about cultural values. Indeed, cultural values still significantly affect the (non)linguistic phenomena of the contemporary Korean business world (e.g., a considerable amount of emotion permitted in Korean companies). Chapters 5 and 6 exemplify the value of affective empathy and sincerity, respectively, in Korean business communication. However, it is true that Korea as a whole is currently undergoing a cultural change. Furthermore, Korean companies are developing their own unique corporate cultures.

Some may argue that cultural differences do not help us get along with each other in the study of cross-cultural communication. This book shows that some business genres are not influenced by culture. For example, a

DOI: 10.4324/9781003108061-8

Korean CEO's online greeting (as examined in Chapter 7) does not illustrate culture-specific features but utilizes linguistic features common to general management that might be found in any CEO's online greeting. In fact, when dealing with cross-cultural data, the role of culture tends to be over-estimated. It is important to remember that proper cultural values should be determined *within context*.

This perspective comes up with Alvesson and Karreman's (2000) conception of little 'd' and big 'D' discourse. Little 'd' discourse represents the textual form of communication, while big 'D' Discourse represents its meaning potentials. On the one hand, little 'd' discourse refers to talk and text in local social interaction. Studies of this type of discourse focus on detailed language in use and talk-in-interaction in specific social contexts. From the tradition of sociolinguistic research, for instance, little 'd' discourse pays attention to linguistic practices, such as the use of pronouns, passive transformation, and nominalization, in order to understand the meaning and interpretation of these linguistic features and the constitutive effects of their use. It also seeks to understand how tones are controlled when sensitive, persuasive, and promotional messages are exchanged internally and externally.

Given this research perspective, this book has exemplified those particular objectives of messages that significantly affect the choice of rhetoric and special management language devices, as discussed in Chapter 7. However, this may not be necessarily consistent with the case involving the perlocutionary force, as demonstrated in Chapters 4, 5, and 6. This exception can be made in big 'D' Discourse. Big 'D' Discourse refers to culturally 'standardized ways of referring to/constituting a certain type of phenomenon' (Alvesson and Karreman 2000: 1134). Discourse is historically formed by myriad local discourses, contingencies, and cultural assumptions that shape social reality (Foucault 1980). It focuses on how it offers linguistic resources for social interaction as it produces its constituting effects rather than its superficial style of communication command. It refers to the 'orders of discourse' – the 'totality of discursive practices of an institution, and relationships between them' (Fairclough 1993: 135). Given the claim, this book has adopted a meaning-centered perspective seeing communication as the 'creation and maintenance of symbolic systems' (Mumby 1988: 5). It equates communication to human interaction, referring to sequenced inter-related acts, the context they create, and the meanings formed at a relational level in linguistic forms. It claims that communication (even written communication) is referred to as the interactional context, and its perception should be duly noted for communication success.

This claim illustrates that text and context should be assigned a prominent role even in the analysis of cross-cultural business communication genres. Interrelationships between text and context focus primarily on text-external properties, viewed as interdiscursive in nature (Bhatia 2010). Interdiscursivity plays an important role in the appropriation of text-external resources across business communication practices. Text-external sources, as mentioned in Chapters 4, 5, and 6, include the conventions that constrain generic constructs and organizational practices. Interdiscursivity is the function of appropriation of generic resources, primarily contextual in nature. It focuses on distinctive relationships between and across organizational practices and organizational cultures. It underpins the importance of context in genre theory. It refers to innovative attempts to create a variety of forms of mixing constructs in appropriating genres.

This book argues that interdiscursivity is central to our understanding of the dynamics of local communication genres, which are used in workplace contexts. It argues for a critical study of discursive features of Korean business communication by focusing on interdiscursivity. Since the text is made possible by a combination of a very complex and dynamic range of resources, besides linguistic conventions as text-internal properties, we should explore multiple discourses that play a significant role in forming specific discursive practices in business communication. The interdiscursive nature of contemporary Korean business communication may also make us rethink how we deal with cross-cultural business communication data. Accordingly, in-depth intercultural studies on cultural values need to be built on the present research undertaken partly from a cross-cultural communication perspective. For pedagogical purposes, besides general aspects of a culture, intercultural business communication instructors need to know what 'appropriate' is in a given business context for effective communication training (Swales 2002).

References

Alvesson, M., & Karreman, D. (2000). Varieties of discourse: On the study of organizations through discourse analysis. *Human Relations*, 53, 1125–1149.

Bhatia, V. (2010). Interdiscursivity in professional communication. *Discourse & Communication*, 21(1), 32–50.

Fairclough N. (1993). Critical discourse analysis and the marketization of public discourse: The universities. *Discourse and Society*, 4(2), 133–168.

Foucault, M. (1980). *Power/Knowledge: Selected Interviews and Other Writings 1972–1977*. New York: Pantheon.

Mumby, D. (1988). *Communication and Power in Organizations: Discourse, Ideology, and Domination*. Norwood, NJ: Ablex.

Swales, J.M. (2002). On models of applied discourse analysis. In C. Candlin (ed) Research and practice in professional discourse (61–77). Hong Kong: City University of Hong Kong Press.

Index